GOOD GOLF
MADE EASY

GOOD GOLF

MADE EASY

FOR THE COMPLETE BEGINNER

TONY DEAR

Commissioned photography
by Bob Atkins

Sterling Publishing Co., Inc.
New York

Library of Congress Cataloging-in-Publication Data Available

10 9 8 7 6 5 4 3 2 1

Published by Sterling Publishing Company, Inc.
387 Park Avenue South, New York, N.Y. 10016
First published in the United Kingdom by
HarperCollins Publishers London

© 2000 by Tony Dear

Distributed in Canada by Sterling Publishing
c/o Canadian Manda Group, One Atlantic Avenue, Suite 105
Toronto, Ontario, Canada M6K 3E7

Sterling ISBN 0-8069-1962-0

CONTENTS

INTRODUCTION

The first time I ever played golf was in my grandfather's back garden with a rusty old 6-iron he kept packed away in his garage. I was six years old. From the moment he handed it to me and showed me how to hold it, I was hooked. The 6-iron has sadly been lost forever, as has the 10-finger baseball grip my grandfather taught me, but my love and enthusiasm for the game of golf is still as passionate as ever. And I fully expect to feel the same way about it in 40 years' time when my grandchildren are hacking my back garden to pieces.

Golf does that to people. It casts a spell. It's claws are stuck in me so deep I will never break free. Great!

In buying this book you are showing early symptoms of a fascination with the game just like mine. You have made a very enlightened decision to risk your mental well being and take up golf. After years of playing, teaching and writing about the game I can assure you there will be times when you want to throw your clubs under the heaviest juggernaut; hopefully those times will be rare, but no matter how frequent or infrequent they are, they will be

eclipsed by the countless occasions when you thank God for the Scots and their bonny idea to hit a ball with a stick through the air towards a hole in the ground.

It won't take long for you to discover that golf isn't as easy as you hoped it might be. In fact it's pretty tricky. The aim of this book is, therefore, to make golf — which some modern day swing 'gurus' (mentioning no names) succeed in over-complicating — sound as easy as possible.

You won't find complex swing theory in these pages. What you will find are the basic fundamentals that are common to all good swings.

But for me the real purpose of this book is to give the beginner, for whom golf might seem unfeasibly difficult at present, a little encouragement. You don't need the perfect swing to play good golf. All you need is enthusiasm and some sound advice on how to get the most out of what talent you have.

This book does not focus solely on technique but discusses other factors that determine your score such as course management and simple psychology, factors which many teachers tend to forget. By the end of it you won't be the proud owner of a swing like Tiger Woods nor will you be able to putt like Brad Faxon or Ben Crenshaw. No book can do that for you. What you should be able to do, however, is enjoy a friendly game of golf without embarrassing yourself or running out of balls.

Mind you, with a little practice and a slice of luck who knows how far you can go? This book should provide an appropriate starting point in your golfing education. After that it's up to you.

Good golfing...

CHAPTER 1

GETTING STARTED

GOLF, LIKE MANY other sports, has a language of its own. Before you get serious about playing the game you'll need to become familiar with some of the odd phrases you are likely to hear at the golf course. Terms like dogleg, cavity back and lateral water hazard will probably mean nothing to you now but by the end of this chapter you should have a good understanding of most of the words and phrases you will hear at some time or other. So before you start to learn how to play golf, take some time to acquaint yourself with the game's vocabulary.

EXPLANATION OF BASIC TERMS

THE GOLF COURSE

TEEING GROUND (OR TEE):

Where each hole starts. The exact position from where you must hit your tee shot is determined by the position of the tee markers. These can be either white, used for men's competitions, yellow, used by men during the week or for non-competitive rounds, or red which are used by lady golfers. You must play your tee shot from a position between the two markers and not more than two club lengths behind them. (The colour of the tee markers may differ from country to country).

FAIRWAY:

The mown strip of grass between the tee and green. Fairways vary greatly in width. At US Open (one of the four Major championships) venues the fairways are

notoriously narrow and often measure as little as 20 yards across. An average fairway at most country clubs and courses in continental Europe, however, will be 40-50 yards wide. It is desirable to find the fairway with your tee shot as controlling the ball from short grass is a lot easier than it is from long grass. Fairways are found on par 4 and par 5 holes (or any hole longer than 250 yards) but not usually par 3 holes where the player is expected to reach the green from the tee.

GREEN: The very closely mown area at the end of the fairway on which the hole is cut. You use a putter on the green as this club has very little loft on the face which helps the ball hug the ground. It is usual for each hole on the course to possess its own green. However, it is not uncommon for two holes to share one green. On The Old Course at St Andrews, for instance, only four holes (1st, 9th, 17th and 18th) have their own. Greens are rarely flat. The vast majority will have some contouring forcing the player to aim his putt away from the hole initially in order for it to curve back as gravity takes effect.

DID YOU KNOW?

In some Middle Eastern countries, where the temperature is too hot for grass to grow naturally, golfers putt on 'browns'. These are areas where the sand has been flattened, raked and coated in oil which hardens to form a smooth putting surface.

FLAG STICK:
The flag stick, or 'pin', shows the precise location of the hole. In Europe, the flags on the front nine holes are usually a different colour to those on the back nine, but in America it is usual for all 18 holes to be yellow. (There are exceptions, of course, such as at Merion Golf Club, near Philadelphia, where oval wicker baskets are used instead of flags).

THE HOLE:
All golf holes are 4.5 inches in diameter and at least 4 inches deep. They are cut with a special hole-cutting device which ensures all the holes on the course are uniform in circumference and depth. Holes can be located anywhere on the green but most clubs will not position any hole less than 8ft from the edge of it.

ROUGH:
The long grass bordering the fairway. The thicker the rough the harder it is to play out of. It is practically impossible to get any control over the ball when you hit out of long rough. The rough at Carnoustie, in Scotland, during The 1999 British Open was heavily criticized for being too penal and the rough at the US Open, shorter but thicker than that at The British Open, often comes under fire from the players too. At your local club the rough is likely to be much less severe but it is best avoided all the same.

SEMI-ROUGH: Some courses have areas of semi-rough located between the fairway and the actual rough. The semi-rough, known simply as the 'semi', is shorter than the rough itself.

HAZARD:

There are two types of hazard; bunkers (shown above) and water features. They are added to a course to makes it visually interesting and prevent it from becoming too easy. You are not allowed to ground your club when addressing the ball in a hazard. If you do you will be penalized two shots.

BUNKER: A depression in the ground filled with sand. The first bunkers on the links courses of Scotland were formed by burrowing animals trying to shelter in the sand dunes from the wind and rain. Nowadays they are cut into the landscape by bulldozers. There is no limit to how big or small they can be. Pot bunkers, like the Road Hole bunker on the 17th hole on the Old Course at St Andrews, are more common on older courses and can be extremely deep, sometimes 10ft. Bunkers on modern courses tend to be much shallower. Some courses like Royal Lytham and St Annes in England possess literally hundreds of bunkers while others, such as Augusta National in Georgia, USA, survive with relatively few. Bunkers are usually sited in close proximity to the green to catch wayward approach shots but fairway bunkers, designed to penalize the inaccurate drive, are common too.

WATER HAZARD: Any lake, pond, ditch, stream, sea or river. There are two types: water hazards and lateral water hazards. A water hazard is defined by yellow stakes and lies across the hole, while a lateral water hazard runs alongside the hole and is defined by red stakes. Water hazards became popular with course designers in the 1920s and 1930s not only because they were visually appealing but also because they served as a source of water with which to irrigate the course. Should your ball land in either type of water hazard you have a number of options for your next course of action (see chapter 9 on Rules).

DOGLEG:

A significant bend in a fairway that can occur on any par 4 or par 5 hole. The majority of holes have some bend in them at some point along their length but for that bend to be regarded as a dogleg it has to be sharp. Some of the most famous holes in the world have severe doglegs. The 13th at Augusta National (below) turns almost at right angles to the left at the halfway point, as does the 17th on the West Course at Wentworth in Surrey, England. Doglegs usually occur at the point where tee shots are expected to finish.

OUT OF BOUNDS (OB):

The Royal and Ancient Golf Club of St Andrews (one of the game's governing body) defines Out of Bounds as ground usually at the edge of the course from which play is prohibited. You are allowed to stand Out of Bounds to play a ball that is in bounds, however. OB can be defined by stakes (normally white), a fence or a line painted on the ground. If your ball lies in an area that is Out of Bounds you must play another ball from as near to the point from which you played your last shot. (For further information on Out of Bounds see chapter 9).

GROUND UNDER REPAIR (GUR):
This is any part of the course that has been damaged. The club committee decides which areas are designated GUR and may prohibit shots being played from within them. Areas of GUR are usually ringed with white paint with the letters GUR clearly written on the line or within the area ringed. If the committee has not prohibited play from within that area you are allowed to play the ball as it lies or you can lift it out and drop nearby (see chapter 9).

LIE:
The term used to describe how your ball is sitting on the ground. A good lie is one where the ball sits up nicely making it easier to achieve good contact . You should always have a good lie if your ball is on the fairway. You will probably have a bad lie, however, any time your ball is in the rough.

EQUIPMENT

TEE:
A tee, or tee peg, is the object upon which you place your ball for the first shot on each hole (known as the tee shot). You are not allowed to tee up your ball for any shot other than the tee shot. It is easier to get the ball airborne off a tee than it is off the ground, especially if you're using a driver or 3-wood, but it is not compulsory. Tees come in various lengths — between one and three inches — and are made of plastic or wood.

BALL MARKER:
When your ball is on the green you are allowed to mark its exact position and pick it up in order to clean off any mud or moisture it may have picked up en route, and to prevent it from interfering with your opponent's/partner's putt. A coin is perfectly suitable for the job. The only time you are allowed to mark your ball and pick it up other than on the green is to identify it as yours when there is any doubt, if two balls have come to rest very close to each other, or to inspect it to see if it is fit for use.

PITCH MARK REPAIRER:
When your approach shot lands on the green it usually makes an indentation. The higher the shot the deeper the pitch mark. You are responsible for repairing it. You should do this to prevent golfers playing behind you from having to putt over the pitch mark. The best tool for the job is a pitch mark repairer which you can buy in the professional's shop, but if you don't have one a tee will suffice. Push the pitch mark repairer, or tee, into the green at the edge of the indentation and push up the turf to make the area flat again.

Pitch mark repairer   Tee   Ball marker

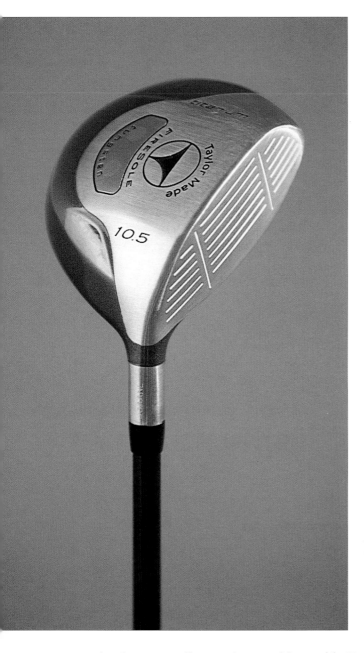

DRIVER:
From the turn of the last century to the early 1980s the heads of drivers (or 1-wood) were manufactured predominantly from persimmon and other laminated woods.

Since the early 1980s, however, persimmon drivers have slowly disappeared to the point where they are now considered collector's items. They have been replaced by metal-headed drivers (still referred to as woods, however). Initially, all metal-headed woods were manufactured from stainless steel but most of today's drivers are made from titanium, a stronger but lighter metal than steel. Because titanium is so much lighter it is possible to make the clubhead bigger thus increasing the size of the sweetspot, the part of the clubface from where the best strike is attained.

You should really only use a driver for tee shots on holes where you need to hit the ball a long way. Do not try to hit a driver off the fairway until you become very, very good at the game. The clubface is too deep — and centre of gravity, in turn, too high — to achieve consistent results. Amateur golfers tend to use drivers with 10 or 11 degrees of loft (the angle at which the clubface is set back from the vertical) on the face. Your driver will probably be the most expensive club in your bag, a top of the range model going for £300-£400 ($450-$600).

FAIRWAY WOODS:
These can be played without a tee off the ground far more easily than the driver and are used for long approach shots —180-230 metres — to par 4s or par 5s. Use one off the teeing ground too, however, if the hole is narrow — a 3-wood is easier to direct than the driver — and if you naturally feel more confident using the 3-wood. A 3-wood has about 15 degrees of loft, a 5-wood 20-21 degrees. Many club manufacturers are also producing 7-woods, 9-woods and even 11-woods which are excellent out of rough.

HEAD COVERS:

You should protect your woods with head covers. Most woods are sold together with their own head cover. If your wood does not come with a head cover, do invest in one. It will protect your club against frost, dirt and scratch marks which will help it fetch a decent price should you ever come to sell it on. A woollen or fabric head cover will cost about £10. Covers for your irons are also available and cost about £10 a set.

Perimeter weighted

Blades

IRONS:

A full set of irons traditionally comprises a 3-iron, 4-iron, 5-iron, 6-iron, 7-iron, 8-iron, 9-iron, pitching wedge (PW) and sand wedge (SW). It is possible to buy a 1-iron or 2-iron for your set but they come separately as so few handicap golfers use them. This is because 1-irons and 2-irons have so little loft it is difficult to get the ball airborne.

A 3-iron has 20 or 21 degrees of loft. The average club golfer will hit one 160-170 metres. The loft on each iron thereafter increases by about 4 degrees per club and each club gets shorter as the number gets higher. Consequently, a 3-iron is designed to hit the ball much lower and further than a 9-iron.

Iron clubs have grooves (shown inset opposite) which are scored on to the face in order to help get the ball airborne and get backspin. To get the best results make sure you keep them as clean as possible by running the sharp end of a tee through them should they clog up with dirt.

There are two main types of iron: perimeter weighted and blades. **Blades** are preferred by some professionals and low handicap amateurs as they are often made from forged steel which gives a softer, more sensitive feel for shots played from around the green. Bladed irons have been around for decades but now are not nearly as popular as **perimeter weighted** irons which were invented in the 1960s and became very popular very quickly. Nowadays well over 90 per cent of sets bought by amateurs are of this type. They are characterized by the large cavity in the back of the clubhead. The weight of the head, rather than being located in the centre as with a blade, is distributed around the edge. This helps the inconsistent golfer achieve good results even when he hits the ball off the toe or heel of the club (the toe is the furthest point of the head from the shaft, the heel is the nearest). If you are new to the game it is highly recommended you play with perimeter weighted irons. A brand new set of irons could cost anything from £200 to £1200, depending, primarily, on who made them.

CLUB	LOFT (DEGREES APPROX)	DISTANCE AM/PRO (METRES APPROX)
3-iron	20	170/200
4-iron	24	160/190
5-iron	28	150/165
6-iron	32	140/165
7-iron	36	130/150
8-iron	40	120/135
9-iron	44	110/120
PW	48	100/110
SW	56	90/100
LW	60	70

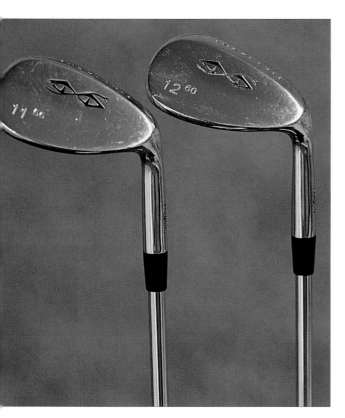

SAND WEDGE:

This club is used predominantly for extricating your ball from sand and is designed especially for this, but you shouldn't restrict its use solely to bunkers. You can use it for high approach shots into the green from 80 metres or so or for pitch shots from around the green. It is the sole of the sand wedge as well as the extra loft that distinguishes it from the rest of the set. The sole is much wider than that of other clubs (the width of the sole is known as the 'flange') and the back edge of the sole is lower than the leading edge, giving the club 'bounce' – the angle between the ground and the line of the sole. This isn't the case with any other club. The bounce allows the sand wedge to splash in and out of the sand rather than bury itself and this makes it easier to get your ball out.

SHAFTS:
It is absolutely essential you get your clubs fitted with the right shafts. The most important property of the shaft is its flex. Ladies', men's regular, stiff, extra stiff and senior shafts are all available today and you simply must have the right shafts if you are to play with any consistency. If your shafts are too flexible you will have trouble keeping the ball straight or on your desired trajectory. Too stiff a shaft on the other hand will make it difficult for you to get the ball up in the air and will also encourage a shot that flies to the right. The other choice to make is which material the shaft is made from. Steel is still the most popular material for shafts in irons but most people these days have a graphite shaft in their driver. That's because graphite shafts are lighter than steel shafts and the lighter the shaft the easier it is to generate clubhead speed.

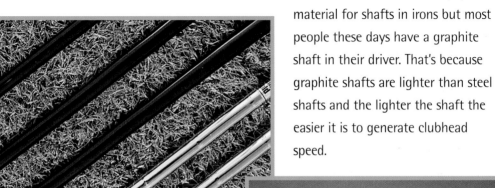

GRIPS:
The vast majority of grips are made from rubber (left and centre) although leather or leather imitation grips (far right) are still available. Rubber grips can be removed and replaced easily and cost about £30 a set. More important than the material of the grip, however, is its thickness. Too thin a grip and your hands will probably be over active in the swing causing you to close the clubface at impact and hit the ball low and left. Grips that are too thick, meanwhile, will prevent a full release of the clubhead, losing you distance and encouraging the ball to fly to the right.

From left to right: the mallet, blade and heel-toe.
Inset: Many putters have soft inserts on the face to improve feel.

PUTTER:

The club used for shots on the green. Putters come in all sizes and shapes and are the most individual club in the bag. There are three main types: the mallet, the blade and the heel-toe.

The mallet, as used in the past by Nick Price and Tom Watson among others, looks bulky but is usually hollow. This allows the golfer to choose the weight of his putter by removing the sole plate and adding or removing small weights. The top of the head usually has several grooves on it which help the golfer align the putter properly.

The blade, just a strip of metal, is the simplest design. The Wilson 8802, a blade putter and one of the most famous putters ever made, was used to great effect by Ben Crenshaw, the 1999 US Ryder Cup team captain.

The heel-toe was the fore-runner to cavity back irons and was invented by Karsten Solheim in the late 1950s. The weight is taken from the centre of the putterface and redistributed to the heel and toe of the club which has the effect of increasing the size of the sweetspot. Thus even if you strike the ball off the heel or toe it should still roll on the intended line. This type is still very popular today but it was probably Seve Ballesteros, who enjoyed great success with it in the 1980s, that bought it to the attention of golfers in Europe.

The broomhandle, the butt end of which fits under the chin, has become popular in the last 10 years. While the left hand holds the top end of the putter tight under the golfer's chin the right hand holds the club half way down and attempts to create a smooth, pendulum like movement of the putterhead. This type of putter has saved the career of many pro golfers, most notably Scotland's Sam Torrance whose putting was becoming ever more shaky with the regular length putter.

GOLF BALL:

Just as the club market has exploded in recent years so has the ball market. Today there is a ball for every occasion, climate, topography and type of player. Choosing which one is best suited to your game can be a complicated process. That said, many club golfers are not sensitive enough to feel much of a difference between them and will stick to the cheapest (you don't want to be losing £3 balls all day after all). Until recently there were, in very basic terms, two types of ball; the two-piece and three-piece. Two-piece balls are still probably the most popular type of ball with amateur golfers. They travel further than three-

These two balls may look the same but they perform differently.

piece balls as a rule and don't cut so easily. They tend to cost less too. Three-piece balls, often made from balata, are generally preferred by professionals because they are softer, have much better feel and a higher spin rate than two-piece balls.

There are no hard and fast rules as to which type of ball you should play. Greg Norman uses a two-piece ball while many amateurs, especially those with low handicaps, prefer three-piece balls with balata covers. As with any piece of equipment testing it out is your best bet for finding the right one for you. Price-wise, a sleeve of three standard two-piece balls will cost £6-7.

SHOES:

This is another area where technology has played a big part in helping to enhance our enjoyment of the game. Gone are the uncushioned, uncomfortable rubber-uppered shoes with the ugly flaps on top (kilties) of yesteryear. The golf shoe of the early 21st century is

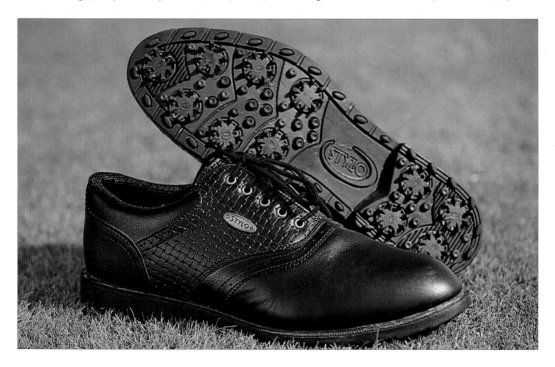

not only comfortable it is waterproof and breathable as well. And in an ever increasing number of cases, it is coming fitted with cleats as opposed to metal spikes. Cleats are made of rubber and cause much less damage to a golf course and, in particular, the greens. There is a question mark, however, over whether or not cleats provide as much grip as spikes in wet and wintry conditions. If your local course is especially hilly and the ground is wet it is probably a good idea to stick to spikes and save the cleats for the spring and summer. A pair of leather upper, waterproof shoes will cost between £50 and £150 ($75-$230).

GOLF BAG:
Every golfer is expected to have a bag in which to carry his/her clubs. A good carry bag will be lightweight (probably made from nylon) but have ample space for clubs, waterproofs, drinks, balls and various other items you may wish to take with you. A quality carry bag costs between £50 and £150 ($75-$230). Trolley bags, for those who prefer to pull their clubs are much larger, heavier and commonly made of leather. They cost £100–£150.

TROLLEY:
Trolleys are used by those for whom 18 holes is too far to carry a heavy set of golf clubs. Most trolleys are collapsible, in order to be able to fit into a car boot easily, and have wide wheels to spread the weight of the bag over as large an area as possible so as not to damage the course. For old or disabled golfers, unable to either carry or pull their clubs, electric trolleys are now available. They are powered by batteries, much like the one in your car, which need re-charging at the end of every round. An electric trolley, including a battery, costs anything between £200 and £500 ($300-$750).

GLOVES:
The majority of golfers wear a golf glove to improve their grip on the club. Right handers wear theirs on the left hand and vice versa. Top quality gloves are made from cabretta leather, which are extremely comfortable but prone to tearing in wet weather. Expect to pay £15. An all weather glove, made from synthetic material, provides better grip in wet conditions and costs less than a leather glove.

WATERPROOFS:
In northern Europe it is a very good idea to have a set of waterproofs handy as playing golf in the rain without any protection from the wet can be a miserable experience. To shield yourself fully you will need both a jacket and a pair of trousers. Gents rain gear is usually navy blue, dark green or black, while ladies can choose from a wider range of colours. Most come with a waterproof guarantee which lasts between one and three years depending on the quality of the garment. Most are breathable as well emitting sweat while the rain is kept out. You can buy a good rain suit for £100 ($150). Top quality suits with lifetime guarantees could cost £250 ($380).

BUGGY:
It is very common nowadays for golf courses, especially those at golf resorts, to provide buggies for hire. In America there are a number of courses which actually forbid walking and insist on the use of a buggy. This practice is, however, extremely rare in Europe. Buggy hire for one round is likely to cost at least £10, although there are some courses that will charge you £20 or £25 ($30-$40).

CADDIE:
The modern day caddie is more than just a simple bag carrier. These days the professional caddie has to calculate the yardage his player has left to the hole, provide encouragement, know what to say and when to say it, be able to take the blame for a bad shot (even if he was in no way to blame for the bad result), tend the flag, and generally act as his employer's right hand man. He is a friend and confidant, diligent, punctual, disciplined and loyal to the end.

With so much golf on television these days the caddies have almost become as well known as the players themselves. Pete Coleman, who has been carrying Bernhard Langer's bag for many years, and Fanny Sunesson who caddied for Nick Faldo before taking on Sergio Garcia's bag for a brief period at the end of 1999, are familiar faces and instantly recognisable to the majority of golf enthusiasts.

SCORING TERMS

ACE: A hole in one.

ALBATROSS: Three under par for a hole. Therefore, a hole in one on a par 4 or a score of two on a par 5.

EAGLE: Two under par for a hole, (a hole in one on a par 3, a two on a par 4 or a three on a par 5).

BIRDIE: One under par for a hole, (a two on a par 3, a three on a par 4 or a four on a par 5).

PAR: The number of strokes in which an accomplished player is expected to complete a hole. Officially, any hole less than 250 yards (about 230 meters) in length is a par 3. A hole between 250 yards and 475 is deemed a par 4 and any hole measuring 476 yards or more is classed a par 5. However, there are some exceptions to this rule.

At Augusta National the 10th hole measures 485 yards but is classed as a par 4 whereas the 13th at just 465 yards is a par 5. This is because the club has taken into account the relative difficulty of each hole, the stroke index. The 10th hole plays downhill all the way making it play a lot shorter than its yardage would suggest. The 13th is a much tougher hole and unlikely to be reached in two shots by the majority of amateur players. It is becoming more common for clubs to award pars based on the difficulty of the hole.

BOGEY: One over par for a hole (a score of four on a par 3 and so on) or a type of competition in which the golfer plays matchplay against the par of the course.

DOUBLE BOGEY: Two over par for a hole.

FILLING IN A SCORECARD

When you play in a strokeplay competition you will be responsible for filling out the scorecard of one of your fellow competitors. You cannot fill out your own for obvious reasons. As you wait to tee off on the 1st hole, fill in your name (Player A), the date, the name of the competition and your handicap at the top of the scorecard before handing it to one of the people you are playing with. Be sure to get your handicap correct. If you get it wrong you could be disqualified from the competition. As you complete each hole, record in the appropriate space the score of the player whose scorecard you are filling in (in the Player A column) and write your own score in the 'marker' column. At the end of the round record the total for all 18 holes and subtract the player's handicap to get the nett score. Next, you must sign your name where it says 'marker's signature' then hand it back to the player. When you get your scorecard back sign your name where it says 'Player's signature' and make sure the person who marked your card has signed it as well. This is most important because you can be disqualified for failing to sign your card.

YARDAGE: The distance from the teeing ground to the front of the green. Note the white teeing markers (the competition tees) are further back than the Yellow's

FILL IN YOUR OWN DETAILS at the top of the card before play starts: the competition, your name, Player A (your partner's name would go in Player B if it was a team competition), the date, and tee time

HANDICAP: the number of shots you are expected to be over par by the end of the round and the number of shots you deduct from your gross score. (A fuller explanation of handicaps can be found over the page)

STROKES REC'D: In most cases the strokes received will mirror your actual handicap. In some competitions, however, the stroke allocation may be less than your handicap

GROSS SCORE for the player of the card you are marking should go here. The score of Player B, where that is applicable, should go in the adjacent column

MARKER'S SCORE: Record your score in here

PAR: the number of strokes an accomplished player is expected to take on each hole – the benchmark for all players

STROKE INDEX: This signifies the hole at which you receive a stroke

POINTS: Space to record the win or loss of a hole, in match-play or, in stableford, to record the points attained. Stableford is a competition popular in Britain where points are awarded to the player based on their score. Pars receive two points, bogeys one, and birdies three

NETT SCORE: The score after handicap deductions

TOTAL GROSS SCORE compiled after totalling each set of nine holes

NETT SCORE after deducting handicap goes here

COMPETITION CLUB CHAMPIONSHIP

Please indicate which tee used

DATE 1/10/2000 **TIME** 9·15 am

	Handicap	Strokes Rec'd	PAR 72 / SSS 72

PLAYER A BOB SMITH — 18 | 18 | PAR 73 / SSS 70

PLAYER B — PAR 73 / SSS 72

Hole	Marker's Score	White Yards	Par	Yellow Yards	Stroke Index	Score A	Score B	Nett Score	W = + L = - H = 0 Points	Red Yards	Par	Stroke Index
1	5	364	4	339	5	6				279	4	9
2	4	424	4	401	1	5				364	4	1
3	3	180	3	159	13	3				159	3	15
4	5	325	4	308	15	5				262	4	13
5	5	495	5	489	17	6				403	5	7
6	5	401	4	370	7	5				370	4	3
7	5	177	3	152	9	4				152	3	17
8	5	505	5	478	11	6				441	5	11
9	4	378	4	347	3	5				298	4	5
		3249	36	3043		45				2728	36	

PLEASE AVOID SLOW PLAY AT ALL TIMES

Hole	Marker's Score	White Yards	Par	Yellow Yards	Stroke Index	Score A	Score B	Nett Score	Points	Red Yards	Par	Stroke Index
10	4	435	4/5	477	4	6				435	5	6
11	5	520	5	494	12	6				440	5	12
12	4	408	4	390	2	5				315	4	2
13	5	405	4	396	8	4				339	4	4
14	4	190	3	165	14	4				165	3	16
15	5	336	4	320	16	5				241	4	14
16	5	485	5	479	18	5				415	5	10
17	3	188	3	141	10	4				141	3	18
18	5	410	4	385	6	5				357	4	8
		3377	36/37	3247	IN	44				2848	37	
		3249	36	3043	OUT	45				2728	36	
		6626	72/73	6290	TOTAL	89				5576	73	

HANDICAP 18

NETT 71

Markers Signature _(signature)_   Players Signature _(B Smith signature)_

Always make sure you sign your card. If you fail to do so, or sign for an incorrect score, you will be disqualified. One of the most recent examples of this befell Irish golfer Padraig Harrington in May 2000. He was leading the Benson & Hedges International by five shots when he was disqualified just before the start of his final round, when it was realized he had failed to sign his card after the first round. So be careful!

HANDICAP

Your handicap is the number of strokes you are allowed to deduct from your gross score — the actual number of shots you take — at the end of each round. Once you have made the deduction you arrive at your nett score, the score that counts in most club competitions. It is a system which allows everyone to play on equal terms. Your handicap is determined by how well you score in competitions and to obtain your first handicap you are usually required to submit to the Handicap Committee three signed scorecards.

GROSS SCORE: The actual number of shots taken on a hole or for the round.

NETT SCORE: The number of shots taken minus your handicap.

STROKE INDEX: Each hole has a different stroke index. The stroke index determines whether or not you receive a shot at that hole. In theory, the hardest hole on the course is stroke index 1 while the easiest is stroke index 18. In a match between an 18 handicapper and a 10 handicapper, the 18 handicapper will receive eight shots from the 10 handicapper (assuming the full difference between the two handicaps is taken). On holes with a stroke index of 1-8 the 18 handicapper will therefore receive a shot and be able to subtract one from his gross score for that hole. Thus, if he scores a five on the stroke index 4 hole, for instance, his nett score will be four.

TYPES OF COMPETITION

STROKEPLAY:
This is the most common form of competition. Each player completes all 18 holes and records the number of shots taken on a scorecard. It is you against the rest of the field. The lowest nett score (gross score minus handicap) wins. Players normally go out in threes (players sometimes go out in twos at professional events). The vast majority of professional tournaments are strokeplay. All four of the professional Majors (The British Open, The US Open, The USPGA and The Masters) are strokeplay tournaments although the USPGA was a matchplay event until 1957.

MATCHPLAY:
This is the original form of competition in which you play a match against one opponent (or two if it's a pairs competition). You start the match all square and the scores for each hole are compared. If Player A wins the 1st he goes 1-up, regardless of how many shots he won the hole by. If Player B then wins the 2nd the match goes back to all square. In matchplay you are allowed to concede your opponent's putt if you think he is unlikely to miss. You win the match when you are up by more holes than there are left. So if you are two holes up with only the 18th left to play you win by 2&1 (two holes up with one to play). Because of the nature of the scoring system, it is quite possible in matchplay for a

player who shoots 68 to lose to an opponent who shoots 73. Matchplay is a very popular form of competition at club level.

FOURSOMES:
Basically, two players in partnership using one ball which they take it in turns to hit. One tees off on the odd numbered holes, the other on the even holes. This can be played under strokeplay or matchplay rules.

FOURBALL:
The same as foursomes only each player plays with his own ball and the better score of the pair is the score that counts.

GREENSOMES:
Both players in a pair drive on each hole. The better of the two drives is selected and the other ball picked up. You play alternate shots for the rest of the hole.

TEXAS SCRAMBLE:
This is a light hearted competition popular with golf societies. You play in a team of two, three or four players. Each player in the team has a ball and drives off. The best of the drives is selected and all the balls in the team are then played from that spot. The process continues until you hole out.

SKINS:
Played by two or more individuals. Each hole has an amount of money up for grabs which you can win only by winning the hole outright. If the best score for the hole is achieved by more than one player the money is carried over to the next hole.

BUYING YOUR FIRST SET OF CLUBS

Once you are fully versed in all the terms related to golf – you should be ready to start playing the game for real. But before that you must have a set of clubs.

Walking into the pro shop or High Street golf store can be like walking into Aladdin's cave. The choice of golf clubs on offer is quite amazing and you'll be forgiven for not knowing where to start. You will soon discover that golf clubs are not cheap and when you're planning to part with this much cash your best plan is to carry out some research. You need to know exactly what you need then decide on a budget and stick to it.

WHAT TO BUY

IRONS: If you are new to the game and buying your first set of clubs it would be extremely foolish to get a top of the range model costing £800 or more. At this stage an £800 ($1200) set will probably be no more use to you than a second hand set costing £100 ($150) that you saw advertized in the local paper. There are no miracle clubs on the market sadly and no matter how technologically advanced a set of clubs is, it will not turn a hacker into a professional. Remember that!

If you are sure you want to play regularly, and have enjoyed a few trips to the local driving range, however, then go ahead and get a brand new set. Buy perimeter weighted irons as they will forgive the off centre strikes you are bound to make. You should be able to find a perfectly good set of irons for no more than £200. Once you have seen a set you like the look of, TRY THEM OUT!!! You simply must hit shots with the clubs before committing yourself. If you can't try them out because the shop doesn't have a testing area, don't buy them. They might look nice but they could feel awful. Ask the professional, or whoever's serving you, if he thinks you need the clubs altered in any way. You may need stiffer shafts than those the clubs are fitted with or, if you're 6'5" tall, you may need them lengthened. Check the grips are the right thickness (they are if they feel comfortable in your hands).

WOODS: The same applies here. Always try them before you buy them. You may benefit from having a titanium headed driver as you will probably hit the ball further with that than with a steel headed driver. Titanium drivers can be expensive, however.

PUTTER: There are no rules here. Try as many as you can and buy the one you hole the most putts with. Simple as that.

BALLS: If you are not a long hitter, you will need a two-piece distance ball. If you do hit the ball a long way but have trouble putting and controlling shots from around the green opt for a softer, three-piece ball.

WHERE TO BUY IT

If you're buying brand new gear there really are only three places to buy it: the professional's shop at the golf course, a High Street golf store or on the internet. Each has its merits. The golf store will probably be able to give you a good deal and a wide choice but it's possible the guy selling you the clubs won't have the slightest clue what he's talking about. You'll get a good price but will you get the right clubs? The same is true of the internet. You'll be tempted by the great prices but once you've received them you've got them for life. The chances of getting the right set of clubs are infinitely better at the pro shop but they may cost you a bit more. You have to decide what your main priority is, your budget or getting the right clubs.

Buying golf equipment is largely about using your common sense. Don't fork out hundreds of pounds if you're going to play five times a year and don't get conned into thinking expensive equipment will turn a bad player into a good one. It won't.

WHERE NOW?

Once you have bought your clubs you are ready to start learning how to play. Don't rush straight out to the golf course, however. Before you do I strongly recommend you pay a number of visits to your nearest public driving range, where it doesn't matter if you strike the ball badly. There, you can practice the fundamental lessons you will read in this book and start to develop your own swing and build a good rhythm without worrying about holding other players up (which you might do on a golf course) or how you're scoring.

It is also wise to book a few lessons with a teaching professional. Most golf establishments from private clubs to public driving ranges have a resident professional who will be available for tuition. Once he and you are confident you can play to a decent standard, go for it! You may have trouble getting a game at a private club but you'll be welcome at any municipally owned or pay and play course.

Pay and play courses can get very busy at times so it's wise to phone a few days in advance to pre-book a tee time. To play at a private club you will normally be asked to prove you have an official golf handicap. Alternatively, you can play as a guest of a member of that club. To become a member of a private club it is usual to be proposed and seconded by two existing members and then interviewed by the club committee.

If you don't know where the nearest golf course to you is located, your local phone directory or Yellow Pages should have the information you need. If that fails you can telephone the official golf association of the country you live in who will be happy to direct you to your nearest golfing facility.

Some courses can get very busy so it is advisable to phone ahead and book a tee time.

THE GOLF SWING

IT'S BEEN SAID that golf is the hardest game in the world to play to a high standard. That may be true but playing to a reasonable standard, one where you can enjoy a round without embarrassing yourself or losing every ball in your bag, is certainly within your capabilities. In fact, if you're in half decent shape, have a modicum of natural ability and are keen to learn, there's no reason why you can't be breaking 100 or, who knows, knocking on 90's door, within a few weeks.

THE FUNDAMENTALS

For most mortals living on Planet Earth, golf is an extraordinarily difficult game that can only get harder by becoming immersed in swing theory. Unlike Nick Faldo, who spent two years dismantling his swing and putting it back together in the mid 1980s under the watchful eye of David Leadbetter, you don't have access to pristine practice facilities, eight hours a day in which to test and perfect your swing, or nearly as technically minded a brain. Faldo thrived on the sort of complex swing theory Leadbetter fed him. It will only tie you up in knots.

In this chapter you are going to learn the fundamentals of the golf swing. These are the positions and movements that are common to all good swings and they are all you need to know at this early stage in your golfing life. Once these fundamentals become second nature to you and you begin to feel comfortable with your new action you will be well on the road to playing good golf.

The very first fundamental all those new to the game are taught is the grip and address position, or how you stand to the ball. Jack Nicklaus, the greatest player who ever lived, had a habit of beginning each new season with a lesson from his teacher Jack Grout in which they concentrated exclusively on these two crucial areas. You may think a guy who won 18 Major championships and countless other pro tournaments would know how to hold a club and stand to the ball. But Nicklaus was aware of the importance of the fundamentals and so should you. Nicklaus and Grout would start by returning to the most basic, but most important, of the fundamentals; the grip. All good swings stem from a good address position and all good address positions start with a good grip.

BUILDING A SOLID GRIP

POSITIONING THE LEFT HAND

1. Position the left hand under the grip so that it runs diagonally across the fingers from the middle of the index finger to the base of the little finger.
2. Wrap your fingers round the grip and fold your hand over the top so that the back of the hand is facing the target. (An inch of the grip should be showing at the top).
3. Make sure the thumb is on top of the grip but slightly to the right of centre as you look down.
4. Pinch the thumb and index finger together.

You should have the feeling the left hand grip is secured by the last three fingers. Also, the tips of those fingers should lightly brush against the fleshy pad at the base of the thumb.

POSITIONING THE RIGHT HAND

1. Again start by positioning the hand under the grip, but this time so that it runs directly across the middle of the fingers.

2. Wrap the fingers round the grip and fold your hand over the top making sure the fleshy pad at the base of the right thumb sits on top of the left thumb and the palm of the right hand is facing the target.

3. The thumb should be on the top of the grip but slightly to the left of centre.

4. Now you have a choice of where to position the little finger of the right hand.

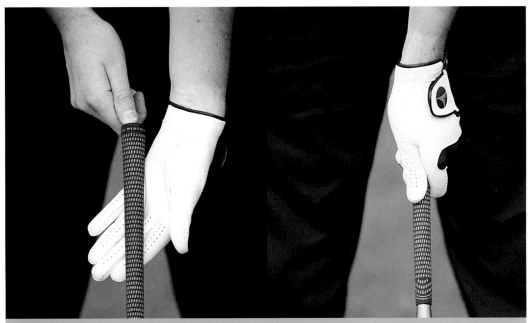

The club runs from the bottom of the little finger through the middle of the index finger.

Wrap the hand over the top of the grip. The back of the left hand faces the target. Thumb just to the right of centre as you look down.

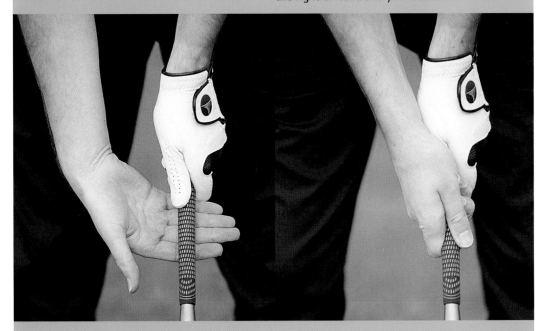

Very much a finger grip. The left thumb fits in underneath the pad of the right thumb. The palm of the right hand faces the target.

To keep your grip as simple as possible just place it alongside the other fingers, below the left hand. That is called the **baseball grip** (all 10 fingers in contact with the club) and is recommended for junior golfers and lady beginners as it provides them with a little extra power. Having said that, many male golfers have experimented with this grip and found it to be the one with which they are happiest. Many swear it helps eradicate their slice, a shot which curves severely to the right.

DID YOU KNOW?
The Vardon grip is named after Harry Vardon, the man who invented it. He was one of golf's first superstars, capturing seven Major titles (six British Opens and one US Open) between 1896 and 1914.

Another option is to rest the little finger in between the index and middle fingers of the left hand and bring the other three fingers higher up the grip. This is known as the **Vardon Grip** and is probably used by 80-90 per cent of the world's golfers. I recommend you give this one a try as it locks the two hands together, allowing them to work as a single, solid unit.

The last option is to interlock the little finger of the right hand with the index finger of the right. Known as the **interlocking grip**, this is the way Tiger Woods and Jack Nicklaus hold the club, so it's not a bad option. People with short fingers tend to favour this method.

Experiment with all three types of right hand grip and adopt the one you feel most comfortable with. The idea is to get your hands working together as a single unit – if they work independently you have little chance of hitting the ball with a clubface that is square to the target – so check there is no gap between your hands.

A good way to ensure the hands are working together is to place a blade of grass or leaf between the left thumb and the pad of the right thumb. It should remain there throughout the

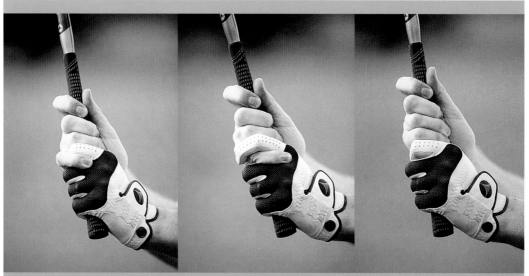

From left to right: The traditional Vardon (overlapping) grip, the interlocking grip, and baseball (10 finger) grip.

swing. Should your right hand come away, your hands will start working independently of each other, the leaf will fall to the ground and you will probably hit a wayward shot.

Whichever grip you do choose, you must hold the club lightly. Not loosely but lightly. The amount of pressure you exert when holding a pencil or the steering wheel of your car is about right for your golf grip.

You should now have what is called a neutral grip. You stand a much better chance of having a square clubface at impact, and thus

Place a leaf between the hands and keep it there throughout the swing. If it falls out your grip is insecure.

hitting a straight shot at the target, if your grip is neutral and the clubface square at address. You can check to make sure your grip is neutral by ensuring the back of your left hand and the palm of your right hand are facing the target. If the back of the left hand and palm of the right face

A strong grip – three to four knuckles visible on the left hand. Back of the left hand facing the sky.

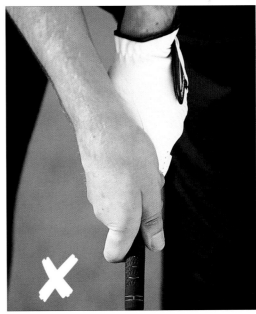

A weak grip – no knuckles visible on the left hand. Back of the right hand almost facing the sky.

This exercise proves the neutral grip is best for the beginner.

upwards then your grip is **too strong** and you are likely to close the face at impact. This will cause the ball to curve to the left, the amount of curve depending on how closed the clubface is. If the back of the left hand and palm of your right hand face downwards your grip is **too weak** and your ball is likely to curve to the right. Many good players, Bernhard Langer and Fred Couples among them, play with a strong grip. Very few succeed with a weak grip. So if a slightly strong grip feels good to you then go with it.

At first, your new grip will feel simply awful. You will ask why you are being instructed to hold the club in such an uncomfortable way and feel inclined to revert to what comes naturally to you. That is perfectly understandable but, sadly, not an option - well not if you want to play consistent golf it's not. You'll find that with a little practice you'll be able to form a neutral grip that feels comfortable without even thinking about it.

WHY A NEUTRAL GRIP IS BEST FOR YOU

Push your hands together (as shown above) and perform a golf swing without a club. You'll discover that as your hands come back to the point where you would make contact with the ball they naturally come back to the same position they were in at the start - back of the left hand and palm of the right facing the target with the fingers pointing straight down. This is neutral. If your grip was too strong and you hands came back to this neutral position at impact then the clubface would no longer be square to the target. It would be closed and the ball would fly left. It's the same with a weak grip only the ball would curve right.

REMEMBER
Grip the club lightly with the back of the top hand and the palm of the bottom hand facing the target.

STANDING TO THE BALL

Once you have gripped the club your next task is to stand to the ball correctly. It is imperative you work hard to achieve a sound address position as the vast majority of bad shots can be traced back to a fault somewhere in your set up. The correct set-up is a combination of good posture, good alignment and good ball position (or where the ball is in relation to your feet).

GOOD POSTURE
Ideally, you need to be relaxed and comfortable but at the same time athletic and primed for action. The position a goalkeeper adopts as he is about to face a penalty or that of a swimmer just prior to diving into the pool is similar to how you should stand to a golf ball.

THREE STEP ROUTE TO PERFECT POSTURE

1. Stand upright with your arms and club held straight out in front of you. Your feet should be shoulder width apart with the toes turned out a little.
2. Bending from the waist bring the club down so the sole sits flat on the ground.
3. Let your arms hang naturally and have the feeling your posterior sticks out a little as you flex your knees. Now get comfortable. A few adjustments here and there won't hurt. Also, lift your chin off your chest.

The importance of good posture cannot be over stressed. Follow this routine and you will achieve it every time. Avoid adopting a posture that is too stooped or too straight (insets).

Good posture will allow you to make a full turn of the shoulders, essential to a powerful swing, and also develop a repetitive rhythm. Follow the three step route to perfect posture until you can get into the correct position without thinking about it.

GOOD ALIGNMENT Before we talk about alignment it is worthwhile explaining a few

simple terms.

Ball to target line: The imaginary line linking the ball and your target.

Inside the target line: The side on which you stand in relation to the ball and the target line.

Outside the target line: Opposite of above.

Square: A term frequently used in relation to the clubface or your stance. Your clubface is square if your feet, knees and shoulders are aligned parallel to the ball to target line and your stance is

square if a line joining your toes runs parallel to the ball to target line.

Open: Your clubface is open if it points to the right of the ball to target line.

Closed: When the clubface points to the left of the target line.

It's no good having a good grip, good posture and a silky smooth swing if you're not aiming correctly. Good alignment is as important to a successful shot as any other fundamental. So make sure you get it right every time.

In order to hit a straight shot at the target you need to have the clubface aimed at the target. In very basic terms if the clubface is facing the target it is aimed correctly. For the more technically minded, if the leading edge of the club is perpendicular to the ball to target line then it is square to the target.

So place the clubface up behind the ball in a position that is square to the target. Then stand in a position that is square to the clubface. If you were to place a club across your toes, knees, hips and, most importantly, your shoulders it

Good alignment means your clubface is aimed at the target and your body is 'parallel left' to that.

would run parallel to the ball to target line, i.e. aiming to a point just to the left of the target. An excellent way to align yourself 'parallel left' is to imagine a train track. You are standing on the inner rail and the ball is on the outer rail which leads to your target. There will be times when you'll want to intentionally curve the ball to the left or right. To do that you will need to align your body differently but we'll deal with that in chapter 7. At this stage you just need to keep it simple. Aim your club and body square to the hole and try to hit a straight shot towards it. Above all, know what it means to be square and seek to be square at all times.

STANCE AND BALL POSITION

Your feet, when hitting a driver, should be slightly more than shoulder width apart and the ball should be opposite your left instep. That gives you a solid base for what is the most powerful swing you will make and it ensures you make contact with the ball just as the driver is beginning to move upwards. That is important as you will maximize your power and hit the ball on the correct trajectory. If the driver was still moving downwards when it made contact you would run the risk of skying the ball straight up into the air.

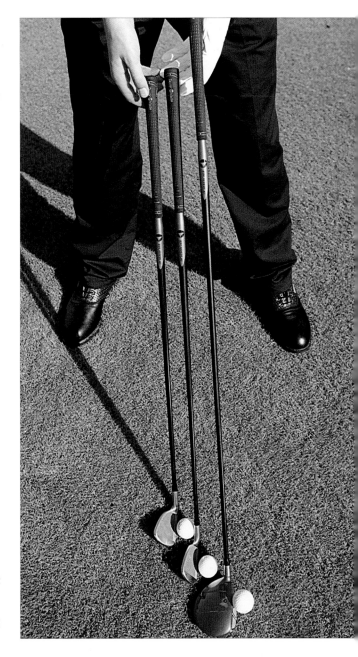

With a driver play the ball opposite your left instep. As the club gets shorter (as shown with the 5-iron and pitching wedge) bring the ball towards the centre and closer to your body.

As the club gets shorter so your stance becomes slightly narrower and the ball moves slightly further back in your stance. So by the time you get down to the pitching wedge (PW) your feet are roughly one foot apart and the ball is midway between your feet. With short clubs such as the pitching wedge, controlling the ball is your main objective. You are not seeking distance but accuracy. To ensure good, crisp contact, which enables you to control the ball better, your swing should be short and crisp as opposed to long and free as it would be with the driver. The narrower stance facilitates this shorter swing and the ball position means the club is still moving downwards as you hit the ball.

That should help put a little spin on the ball, giving you better control.

Many beginners worry about how far they should stand from the ball. A distance that feels comfortable is the easy answer. But bear the following in mind: obviously, the longer the club is the further you should stand from the ball. For every club, however, your arms should hang naturally, the sole of the club should be flat on the ground and there should be a gap of about five or six inches between your hands and left thigh. That will give your hands the room to swing through the impact zone without being hampered by your body. Again, after a little practice you will begin to stand the correct distance from the ball without conscious effort.

SUMMARY
Never underestimate the importance of standing to the ball correctly.

At address the butt of the club should be about five-six inches from your left thigh (a fist's width.)

BASIC CHECKLIST?

Grip
- Back of left hand and palm of right facing target. ✔
- Grip in the fingers of both hands. ✔
- Light grip. No tension in the forearms. ✔

Posture
- Stand tall. No slouching. ✔
- Knees flexed. ✔
- Chin off chest. ✔

Ball position
- A comfortable distance away from you. ✔
- Opposite the left instep for the driver, in the middle for a pitching wedge or sand wedge. ✔

Alignment
- Clubface facing directly at the target. ✔
- Body aligned parallel left of the ball to target line. ✔

Get the address position right. Faults at address will lead to further faults as the swing gets underway.

Do it right and you're well on the way to hitting a great shot. Get it wrong, however, and the chances of making good contact and sending the ball to the desired location

become very slim indeed. So before you even begin to learn how to actually swing the club make absolutely sure your address position is as near to perfect as you can make it.

THE GOLF SWING

In order to give you a good idea of the sort of positions your club and body should be in at various stages of the swing, it is helpful at this early stage to break it down.

Always remember, however; the golf swing is called a swing for a very good reason. It should flow. It should not be a staccato sequence of set positions you check off as you reach them. It is vital you appreciate the fact that good rhythm will make up for faults in your technique but good technique is useless without good rhythm.

It is also important to note that seeking perfection will cause you much distress. No one, not even Tiger Woods, possesses the perfect golf swing – Woods is pretty close, of course – and searching for it will prove a futile exercise right from the start. Lee Trevino, one of the greatest players that ever lived, has a swing that would be described as unconventional by the most kind hearted of onlookers. The less polite would have no hesitation in saying it was downright ugly. And other highly successful, modern day players like Jim Furyk, Justin Leonard, Scott Hoch and John Daly don't exactly have text book swings either.

So don't be concerned if your swing looks different from the one shown here (it's far from perfect too!). As long as you get the fundamentals right and swing the club with a rhythm that feels natural and repeats shot after shot you will progress as a golfer.

An elegant swing is not essential – just make sure the fundamentals are right.

The correct takeaway. Low and slow.

Top: Outside the target line.
Above: Too far inside the target line.

THE TAKEAWAY

The golf swing is a chain reaction and as with all chain reactions its first movement is its most influential. It is crucial you move the clubhead away from the ball in the correct manner if your top of the backswing position is to be correct. Likewise your top of the backswing position must be right if you are to deliver a square clubface powerfully into the ball.

A baseball pitcher generates speed by allowing the wrists to hinge and release (left). You will never generate power if your arms are rigid and tense (right).

The backswing exists purely as a tool to put the club in the correct position at the top from which to attack the ball and also to build up power. You do not hit the ball with your backswing. So go easy. Quick, jerky movements caused by too tight a grip and a build up of tension in the forearms will actually prevent you from storing up any power and give you little chance of hitting an accurate shot.

Taking the club away from the ball should be a slow and deliberate motion. The wrists do not break and the club remains low to the ground. In fact, the 'Y' shape formed by your arms and the club when you addressed the ball remains pretty much intact.

Take the club back straight. Do not push it outside the ball to target line or bring it back on the inside. Don't strain your body either. Try to retain exactly the same posture you had at address, maintaining the flex in the knees and the angle of your spine.

HINGE THE WRISTS
Power in the golf swing comes from a combination of your upper body turning against the resistance of the lower body – the hips and knees staying relatively quiet – and the hinging and unhinging of your wrists. You must incorporate both if you are to hit the ball a long way. It is no good having a full upper body turn if your wrists remain locked.

When the left arm is parallel to the ground the club should point to the sky.

To achieve a good shoulder turn visualize your back turning to face the target.

Likewise you will never hit a powerful shot if you rely solely on your wrists.

Hinging and unhinging the wrists is an important movement in many sports. Think of how a tennis player whips a fast, dipping, top spin shot, cross court. Or imagine the fast bowler in cricket or pitcher in baseball almost flicking his wrist as he lets go of the ball to give it a little extra pace. It is the same in golf. If you maintained the 'Y' shape formed by arms and club shaft all the way to the top of the backswing you would put serious strain on your back and you would not create any power. You need to have that movement of the wrists if you are to maximize the distance you hit the ball. And it is now in the swing, after the initial takeaway, that the wrists begin to hinge. When your left arm is parallel to the ground the club should be pointing to the sky. That is as much as they need to hinge. Any more and your grip may begin to slacken and you would lose control of the club. If this position comes naturally to you then lucky old you. If not, stand in front of a mirror and get into the position over and over again until it does come naturally. Believe me, it will pay very handsome dividends.

SHOULDER TURN – COIL

As I mentioned above, the ability to hinge your wrists must be accompanied by a turn of the upper body if you are to build a powerful swing. The body must NOT move to the right laterally (called a sway) a significant distance. An inch or two won't hurt, a foot or more will. An excellent way to turn your upper body successfully is to focus on the movement of the left shoulder. As your backswing progresses the left shoulder turns under your chin. At the top of the backswing it sits directly beneath it. Another good way to visualize the body turn is picture your back turning to face the target. That might be beyond some whose back simply won't allow them to turn this far. That's okay. Turn as far as you can until you start to feel the strain.

There are scores of top professionals in the world today who are sufficiently supple to turn their shoulders through more than 90 degrees while maintaining good rhythm and balance. Tiger Woods has no trouble getting past that point and Ernie Els is another who has the ability to turn his shoulders a long way but keep his hips and knees relatively free of movement. John Daly's back is so malleable he can turn his arms so that his hands are directly above his head but

the player with perhaps the most impressive shoulder turn in the game today is Sergio Garcia, the 20-year-old wonder kid from Spain. It is very unlikely you will be able to turn your shoulders like he does but a few stretching exercises every day, working on loosening up your back, will certainly help.

WEIGHT SHIFT

Shifting the weight of your body in the golf swing correctly is vital. In short, as you bring the club back your weight should move back with it on to your right foot. And as the club comes back down so the weight moves forwards on to your left foot. This movement of the weight again ensures maximum power and the correct angle of attack into the ball. Many beginners get this important lesson wrong by shifting their weight in the wrong direction. They move forwards then backwards. This is called a reverse pivot and it can lead to any shot under the sun, although rarely a good one. Others overdo it by throwing their weight recklessly on to the outside of their back foot in the backswing then forwards on to their front foot in the downswing. This again leads to a total loss of control.

The feeling should be of your weight coming back naturally on to the instep of your right foot as the club comes back, then moving smoothly on to your left foot as you swing through to a balanced finish.

Weight too much on the left foot at the top of the swing (above) and pushed back on to the right foot in the follow through (left) – the classic reverse pivot.

TOP OF THE BACKSWING

A lot of amateur golfers are prone to collapsing their arms at the top. The left arm bends excessively (it is a myth that the left arm should remain straight. It should not be too crooked either, however) and the hands drop down with the club almost coming to rest on the back of the neck. This will result in a shot that is neither powerful nor accurate.

You should get the feeling the hands are as high above your head as is comfortable and, even more importantly, **as high as you are able to get them while maintaining the same body angles you created at address.** This last point is critical. You must retain the angle of your spine and the same amount of flex in your right knee (right handers) that you created at address. If you straighten your body your head inevitably rises which means you have to drop it again in the downswing if you are to make good contact with the ball. Conversely, if you stoop over more when taking the club back, your head dips and you have to raise it in the downswing. That will

never lead to any consistency, which can only be achieved if your head remains relatively static. Many good players will deliberately move their chin very slightly to the right in the backswing to ease the turning of the shoulders and to get the feeling they are 'loading up' behind the ball, but not one will raise or drop his head consciously. As for how far the club should go back you will inevitably lose control of it if it goes past the horizontal (parallel with the ground). Even when hitting a driver the horizontal should be your absolute limit. John Daly takes it back much further than that but his back is infinitely more supple than yours and his natural timing a good deal more refined. The swing for an iron club should fall short of the horizontal. This increases your control over the clubhead, just what you need for crisp, accurate approach shots.

Club: short of parallel with the ground

Hands: high

Wrists: hinged

Head: on the same level as it was at address

Shoulders: turned 90 degrees

Right knee: still flexed

Weight: on instep of back foot

REMEMBER

Take the club back slowly and turn your back on the target, maintaining the flex in your right knee.

DOWNSWING

THE TRANSITION

As with the takeaway at the start of the backswing, it is absolutely vital you start the downswing smoothly. Many amateur golfers make the transition from backswing to downswing a hurried, jerky action and lose their rhythm, thus giving themselves little chance of hitting a solid shot. You should, ideally, have the feeling you start down with the same tempo as you started back. This should prevent you from 'coming over the top', a common problem with handicap golfers. Coming over the top involves throwing your elbows, hands and the club out in front of you as you start down. The right elbow flies away from your body and you bring the club into the ball from way outside the ball to target line. Your swing therefore becomes a sort of figure of eight motion – inside on the way back, outside on the way down. This is how 99 per cent of slices occur.

THE RIGHT ELBOW

An excellent way to prevent that figure of eight motion and to get the club coming back to the ball from slightly inside the target line is to have the feeling that your right elbow tucks into your side in the downswing.

WEIGHT SHIFT

As the club comes down your weight moves from your back foot on to your front foot so that by the end of the swing virtually all your weight is focused on the front foot. If you have a picture in your mind of how you should look at the end of the swing (front foot on the ground, sole of the back foot off the ground and facing behind you) this will help you shift your weight forwards. A lot of amateur golfers have a problem shifting their weight forwards in the downswing. They get stuck on the back foot

Keep the transition smooth. Just let your arms drop naturally into the hitting zone and keep your head behind the ball.

where most of their weight remains until well after they have hit the ball. If you are like that it is a good idea, next time you practice, to actually lift your back foot off the ground as you swing through to a finish.

HEAD BEHIND THE BALL
Your head must be behind the ball as you make contact. If it moves ahead of the ball it becomes difficult to square the clubface. It is only after you make contact that your head moves slightly ahead of the position in which the ball had been.

HIP ACTION
Your hips, which should have been square to the target at address, open up as the club comes down. DON'T make a conscious effort to do this as it should happen naturally. If you keep your head behind the ball as you approach impact your hips are unlikely to slide forward as you come down, a fault that can lead to horrendous results. As you are learning and developing your swing, however, a good image to develop in order to get the hip action correct is of someone behind you pulling your right hip backwards in the backswing and your left hip backwards in the downswing.

THE IMPACT POSITION

Head: behind the ball, eyes still fixed on the ball

Wrists: fully unhinged

Weight: 70-80 per cent on your front foot, heel of back foot slightly off the ground

You will hear some people say the impact position should be a mirror image of the address position. It is close certainly, but not identical. At address your weight should be balanced between your two feet, but by the time you hit the ball about 70-80 per cent of your weight will be on your left foot.

The feeling you should get is of hitting 'through' the ball, not 'at' it. Imagine the ball is simply getting in the way of your smooth, fluid swing. Do not try to get back down to the ball as quickly as you can. Simply unwind smoothly and let the ball get in the way of the clubhead.

REMEMBER
Don't be in a hurry to get back to the ball. Move your weight smoothly on to your left foot keeping your head behind the ball.

THE FOLLOW THROUGH

THE RELEASE

Releasing the club correctly through the impact zone adds to your power and virtually ensures the ball sets off in the desired direction. If you fail to release the clubhead you promote a pushy, steering movement which greatly reduces your power and sends the ball, more often than not, to the right. It should be a similar movement to that of tennis players who release the racquet head when hitting a top spin forehand shot. It is a matter of letting the wrists go and should happen naturally as your body unwinds in the downswing. Really, you can only prevent a powerful release of the clubhead if you grip the club too tightly or

DID YOU KNOW?

The average amateur golfer swings his driver at somewhere between 80 and 90mph. Powerful professional golfers such as Tiger Woods and John Daly average about 115-120mph but the quickest of them all is World Long Driving champion, Jason Zuback, from Canada, whose clubhead speed has been clocked at 168mph.

consciously try to hold the club off by 'steering' the ball towards the target.

If you feel you are having problems releasing the clubhead try to make contact between the insides of your forearms after contact is made.

EXTENSION

You must not wrap your arms around your body after impact. They must extend fully towards the target. To hit the ball powerfully the clubhead should be in contact with the ball for as long as possible. Obviously, we are talking about thousandths of a second here but a small amount either way makes a lot of difference. By extending the clubhead down the line as far as is comfortable – but keeping your head behind the position the ball was in – you will help the transfer of power stored up in the backswing through the ball and go a long way to starting the ball off in the right direction.

Extend your arms towards the target and allow your head to rise naturally.

THE FINISH

Absolutely the most important characteristic of the finish (shown opposite) is balance. You must be able to hold the position you finish in at least until the ball lands. A balanced finish where all your weight in focused on the front

> **REMEMBER**
> Maintain a good rhythm throughout. Finish in a balanced position with the sole of the back foot facing behind you and your waist facing the target.

foot with the sole of your back foot facing behind you is testament to a smooth and unhurried swing. And as you well know by now, swinging the club smoothly and unhurriedly is the only way you are going to play successful golf.

SUMMARY OF THE GOLF SWING

You have learnt an awful lot over the last few pages. It probably all sounds a little technical at present, but don't despair. The longer you play the game and the more you refer to this book, the more you will understand and be able to implement. The aim of giving you so much information is to give you something to refer to and compare your swing with when piecing it together. I use the phrase 'piecing together' very reluctantly as it gives the impression the golf swing is a sequence of set positions you must get into if you are to succeed. As you read earlier in this chapter, however, that is definitely not the case. **Your golf swing must flow.** It must start and finish smoothly with the club reaching its top speed as you hit the ball not by conscious effort but simply due to the smooth unwinding of your body from the top of the backswing.

Acknowledging this is a very important step in your education as a golfer.

ABOVE ALL, WORK ON THE MOST BASIC FUNDAMENTALS!

THESE ARE: From a sound address position take the club away slowly. As the swing progresses coil your body up like a spring by turning your left shoulder under your chin and your back to the target but keeping your knees relatively quiet. Shift your weight on to your back foot. **Complete your backswing.** That means getting to the top without feeling a sudden compulsion to change direction. Make the transition from backswing to downswing smooth. Do not thrash at the ball wildly from the top. Maintain your spine angle and the flex in your knees and let the ball get in the way of the clubhead. Extend your arms through the ball and finish balanced with your waist facing the target.

THINK: COIL, UNWIND, BALANCE.

Never get bogged down in technique or over complicate matters when you are on the golf course. Rely on your natural ability and what you have grooved. Work on what is not grooved on the practice ground.

Head: has now lifted naturally so you are able to watch the flight of the ball. It has not remained down

Right shoulder: has passed the chin

Back: fairly straight up and down, definitely not bent back into a reverse 'C' position

Waist: facing the target. Trying to finish in a position where your upper body faces the target encourages the correct body rotation

Weight: almost totally on front foot

From start to finish the golf swing should be a free-flowing motion.

RHYTHM AND TEMPO

Perfecting all the fundamentals you have learnt will mean nothing if you don't swing with rhythm. Good rhythm gives you a better chance of controlling the ball and hitting it further. All the great swingers have great rhythm. Nick Price's tempo is quicker than most but it's natural to him and, importantly, the same whichever club he is using. You'll notice if you watch

No hint of a grimace or lunge for the ball. Swing smoothly and you will achieve solid contact more often.

the great players that none of them exert any great effort when swinging a golf club and yet the ball flies off like a rocket when they hit it. **They achieve effortless power, not powerless effort.**

Great rhythm means swinging within yourself. It allows you to hit the ball out of the sweetspot of the club, and thus control the flight of the ball, more often. You should feel you swing a pitching wedge at the same tempo you swing a driver. The ball goes further when you hit a driver because the club is longer, has less loft and your swing is longer. To keep the game simple – our number one objective – feel as though you have one golf swing, not 13 different swings for the 13 different long clubs in your bag (a putter brings you up to the permitted 14). The only conscious difference between hitting a wedge and a driver should be where you position the ball in your stance and how far you stand from it. This will help you develop a constant rhythm for every club in the bag.

THE LADY GOT RHYTHM

Ernie Els, Nick Faldo, Steve Elkington, Ian Woosnam, David Duval and countless other golfers on the men's tour all possess great rhythm but the golfer with perhaps the sweetest rhythm in the game is, in fact, a woman. Annika Sorenstam of Sweden, who won back to back US Women's Opens in 1997 and 1998, swings a golf club so smoothly and effortlessly she doesn't actually appear to be trying. She stands at just 5'6" and can't weigh much more than a full bag of clubs and yet she can hit drives of 250 yards with great regularity. It all comes from perfect timing, something that would not be possible without the easy, repetitive rhythm she developed as a teenager.

3

PRACTICING YOUR GOLF SWING

PRACTICING ANY DISCIPLINE can be excruciatingly dull at times and golf is no exception. Banging range balls into a field all day will become tedious if you don't vary your routine with a few entertaining drills to alleviate the monotony. A good practice drill is fun to do, simple to get right, but most importantly, effective.

PRACTICE WITH PURPOSE

While regular practice is an essential part of maintaining an effective golf swing, you will derive no benefit from practicing for the sake of it. It is counter productive to aimlessly bang balls on a driving range. You must always practice with purpose and that means aiming at a target. Practice doesn't need to be boring. An enjoyable drill will stimulate your desire to practice and help groove the part of the swing you are working on. Here are 10 of the best.

1. HIP DRILL
works on:
Correct hip action. A lot of amateurs tend to slide the hips back then forwards, rather than rotate them. This has several undesirable effects. Firstly, in the backswing, it pushes your weight on to the outside of your back foot. This can play havoc with your balance and severely reduce your chances of making solid contact. Secondly, it makes it more difficult to achieve a full shoulder turn and the swing becomes a lateral movement sideways rather than a turn and coil. This loses you a lot of power. Thirdly, your head inevitably moves backwards too. Your head should ideally be pretty still, an inch or two's movement to the right (right handers) is okay to encourage the shift of weight on to the back foot. Any more is potentially dangerous. Lastly, if then you slide forwards your head gets ahead of the ball before you make contact. This too loses you power and is likely to result in a block that goes straight right.

An excellent drill for improving your hip action and keeping your body behind the ball.

Right: Pushing the umbrella away slowly will help you develop a better takeaway.

how to do it right:

Stick an umbrella in the ground tight up against the outside of your left foot. When you swing the club don't allow your hips to make contact with, or knock over, the umbrella. In order to prevent contact between your hips and the umbrella your hips have to rotate anti-clockwise in the downswing.

2. THE UMBRELLA works on:

Slow takeaway. Too many club golfers ruin their chances of making a smooth swing and hitting a good shot by jerking the club away from the ball. Their first motion is hurried and there is no harmony in their swings between the arms and body. The swing must start smoothly and slowly, the hands and body working in unison to help build up the power.

how to do it right:

Position an umbrella up against the back of your club as you address the ball. Then simply move the umbrella away from you as you bring the club back. It should move slowly along the ground. Your whole body responds to

the umbrella's resistance by slowing down and working as a single powerful unit rather than several destructive ones working in opposition to each other. Your wrists become less active and the emphasis is put on the big muscles making the powerful coil of the body you need to make in order to hit the ball a good distance.

3. THE BUCKET OF BALLS
works on:
Keeping the clubface square throughout the swing. There is a great temptation for many amateurs to fan the clubhead open as they bring the clubhead away from the ball. It feels like a powerful move because they sense they will need to flip the wrists back in the opposite direction later in the swing. It may add a few yards to some of your shots if you time it right but that won't happen with any great consistency. The clubhead should really be square throughout the entire swing and your hands should not twist if you are to deliver a square clubface to the ball on a regular basis.

how to do it right:
Take up your address position but instead of holding a golf club hold a bucket of range balls like this (the bucket should be straight up and down, not tilted). As you turn back to halfway keep the bucket straight up and down with the open end continuing to face upwards. None of the balls should fall out of the bucket. This represents a square clubface (back of left hand facing in front of you). If you tilt the top forwards the balls will obviously fall on to the ground. This represents a closed clubface (back of the left hand facing to the ground). If

This will help you understand when the clubface is square. Letting a few balls go indicates a good release.

the balls fall out of the bucket behind you it means your hands have, in effect, opened the clubface (back of the left hand facing the sky). It is the same for the follow through. As you swing past the imaginary impact position a few balls may leak out of the bucket because of the acceleration in your swing. The top of the bucket continues to face upwards.

This drill demonstrates very well the relationship between the back of the left hand and the position of the clubface. At address the back of the left hand faces the target, halfway back it should face in front of you while halfway through it should face behind you.

4. FEET TOGETHER
works on: Balance and rhythm.
This drill is an absolute beauty and one you can't use too often. It works on virtually every part of your swing, the end result being a smooth, balanced action and better ball striking. As we have discussed too many new golfers develop quick, jerky swings as they believe the quicker they swing the club back the further they will hit the ball. Their takeaway is over in a flash and

Go easy. Swing too quickly and you could fall flat on your face.

they are in such a hurry to get back to the ball from the top of the backswing they lose all their rhythm, tempo and balance. This drill will put a stop to that.

how to do it right: Stand with your feet together and hit a few shots trying to
maintain your balance. It will be difficult at first as you are so used to having your feet further apart but the more you do it and the more you slow your swing down, the easier it becomes. Use no more than an 8-iron to begin with. You will notice this drill has a dramatic effect on your hip action too. If you're a slider you will no longer be able to sway backwards then forwards as you would inevitably fall over if you did.

5. COMMITMENT BUILDER
works on:
Making sure you totally commit yourself through impact and extend fully through the ball. A major fault of many amateur golfers is their inclination to 'come off' the shot. This simply means not committing yourself all the way through the impact zone. Contact, after this fault has occurred, is rarely solid. This basic drill is an effective way of improving your impact position and encouraging you to extend through the ball.

how to do it right:
Just place a tee 15cm in front of your ball (using a driver) and imagine you are trying to hit another ball off that tee.

6. PATHFINDER
works on:
Establishing the correct path of the clubhead in the takeaway and approaching impact. As you discovered in chapter 2, the golf swing is a chain reaction. If the outcome of the chain reaction is going to be positive then the first link in that chain has to be correct. This drill will ensure you start the club back on the correct path — neither too far inside nor outside the target line. In addition to that it will also ensure you bring the club back to the ball on the correct path — again, straight down the target line.

Above: Imagine you are hitting a ball off the second tee.

how to do it right:
Place two tees in the ground 20cm behind the ball and about 15cm apart. One should be on the outside of the ball, the other on the inside. Swing back and through avoiding the tees.

Above: The Pathfinder drill is a great way to encourage the correct swing path.

7. PUMP THE ARMS

works on: Eliminating the hit from the top. This drill is another powerful weapon in the fight against this common fault. It too will help get the club coming down into the ball on the inside and prevent you from lunging at it which throws your golf swing out of sync and forces your head to get ahead of the ball. In basic terms this drill will work wonders for your rhythm and greatly improve your impact position.

how to do it right:

Make a slow swing but stop halfway down and pump your arms up and down three times before hitting the ball and completing the swing.

Pumping the arms is a great way to get the club coming down on the inside and preventing the hit from the top.

A powerful golf swing needs a solid base. Limit the movement of your knees with this drill.

Don't worry if you make a bad contact. It will take a few goes before you hit the ball solidly. Again, use no more than an 8-iron. You are trying to develop rhythm, not hit the ball a mile.

8. BALL BETWEEN THE KNEES
works on:
Solid, stable leg action. Amateurs often run away with the idea that if their legs are very active they will create more power. Nothing, well very little, could be further from the truth. A powerful golf swing needs a solid base. Ideally, your centre of gravity should remain stable during the swing. Excessive movement in the legs will cause your head to rise and dip, your centre of gravity to leap about all over the place and your balance to be lost.

how to do it right:
Just make a few swings with a ball between your knees. You will notice your knees are forced to remain still. They simply cannot kink inwards or outwards – a sign of an unstable swing. And again, you will discover this drill has plenty of desirable side effects. Your hip turn will improve as you will find it hard to sway backwards and forwards. You will have to swing slowly too, so your tempo will benefit.

9. THE LINE OF BALLS
works on:
Rhythm. You will have noticed the majority of these drills seek to improve that particular aspect of your swing. I make no apology for that. Good rhythm is so important to your swing. In fact, a swing that isn't technically sound but has great rhythm is better than a sound technique with no rhythm. So work on it. Try this drill at the start of your practice session to get your muscles working and your body attuned to a good tempo.

Don't hesitate at any point. Just walk down the line of balls continuously swinging the club.

how to do it right:
Tee up 10 balls about a foot from each other. Then simply walk down the line of balls without stopping at any point to regrip the club or get into your address position. You will soon discover the need for performing this drill slowly. Quick, jerky movements will lead to disaster.

10. SWING ONE HANDED
works on:
Timing. Timing is controlling the motions of your body and club to create the optimum effect. Timing the ball well will send it a long way. If your timing is out slightly, however, you will lose distance and control. Good timing in the golf swing is dependent on many factors one of the most important of which is the movement of the right arm in the downswing.

The separation of the right hand away from the right shoulder will help prevent the move 'over the top' and generate more power.

DID YOU KNOW?

Bruce Lietzke, a successful player on the US Tour for many years in the 1980s and 90s, was not known for his desire to practice. To demonstrate just how little he did visit the practice range his caddie placed a banana skin in the headcover of his driver at the end of one season. On the 1st tee of Lietzke's first tournament the following year the caddie removed the headcover from the driver only to discover the banana skin was still there. Lietzke had not played a single shot for months.

One of golf's most famous coaches, David Leadbetter, with Greg Norman.

At the top of your backswing your right arm is bent. But it has straightened by the time you come to hit the ball. The point at which the arm becomes straight is critical. If it releases too soon you will throw the club out to your right and lose all the potential power that comes from the unhinging of your wrists at impact. One of the best ways to develop the correct movement of the right arm is with this drill.

how to do it right:
Swing a club with only your right hand. Simplify it at the start by cutting the heads off a few daisies but as you get used to the motion and become more confident try hitting a golf ball. It is very difficult to begin with so expect to hit a few shanks and tops at first. After 10 or so attempts, however, your body will become attuned to the task and start releasing the right hand at precisely the right time, thus achieving good contact. Do it many times to develop the correct release of the right arm.

QUANTITY ISN'T NECESSARILY CORRECT

Vijay Singh of Fiji practices more than any other man on the planet. Whenever he isn't actually playing he's practicing. Colin Montgomerie, on the other hand, rarely practices, choosing to rely on instinct instead. Both are phenomenally successful golfers — Singh has won several tournaments on both the US and European Tours including the 1998 USPGA Championship and 2000 Masters while Montgomerie has been the number one money earner in Europe for seven straight seasons. But they have developed totally different practice routines to bring them up to 'racing speed'. Singh would not survive long on Tour were he to visit the practice ground as infrequently as Montgomerie who, in turn, would quickly grow bored of the game if he copied Singh's routine. You have to work out the amount of practice that is right for you. Don't think that quantity is necessarily a good thing but don't turn down the opportunity to practice whenever you can, either.

AROUND THE GREEN

WHEN MOST AMATEUR golfers go to the driving range to practice they take with them a driver and a selection of irons. They then bash balls as far as they can with each club for upwards of an hour. Surprisingly, no thought whatsoever is given to pitch shots, chip shots or bunker play. And yet it is the short game, the shots played from around the green, which can, potentially, have the most profound effect on their score and, consequently, their handicap. The short game is an immensely important department of your game, so never take it lightly.

THE SHORT GAME

The importance of the short game cannot be over-emphasized. Often the only difference between a 15-handicapper and a 10-handicapper is the 10-handicapper's ability to get down in two shots from just off the green.

Imagination and natural feel are, of course, important to anyone's short game but don't assume you will fail to get up and down every time if you believe you have neither. The more you practice the quicker you will develop a feel for the short game and the more you will discover about the versatility of each of your clubs.

There are two basic shots that every beginner needs to develop a good feel for if he is to perform well from around the greens; the lofted pitch and the chip and run (also known as the bump and run).

50-100 YARDS   THE LOFTED PITCH SHOT

This is a lofted shot, played with a sand wedge or pitching wedge from anywhere between 50 and 100 yards. Because the ball flies relatively high it stops quickly after landing so aim to pitch the ball close to the hole.

The set-up Remember, when you are this close to the green it really isn't distance you need but control. So feel the desire for control as you address the ball rather than the desire to hit the ball as far as you can. As with all 'control' shots like this you want to hit down on the ball so position it towards the back of your stance. Grip down a couple of inches on the handle too.

There should be a little more weight on your left foot than your right foot and your stance should be open a little to give you a good view of the line of the shot.

A common fault among beginners is to adopt a stance that is too similar to their set-up for a full shot. Their feet are too wide apart and are often too square to the hole.

Above: Walk ahead and pick a point where you want to land the ball.

Right: Ball back, hands forward, feet together.

The swing
The swing is predominantly a movement of the upper body — your shoulders, torso and arms. Think 'back and through' to maintain a good rhythm and focus on making a crisp contact with the ball by making sure your hands are ahead of it at impact and holding the club off a little (palm of your right hand still facing the sky after impact,

Hinge your wrists, keep your head still and be firm through the ball.

THE MIZE EFFECT

The 1987 US Masters was decided in a play-off between Seve Ballesteros, Greg Norman and Larry Mize – two of the sport's biggest names against a comparative unknown. After Ballesteros bogeyed the 1st extra hole, the 10th, to drop out Mize and Norman were left to battle it out for the Green Jacket (traditionally given to the winner of the Masters). At the next hole, Mize hit a dreadful approach shot way right of the green, leaving himself a tricky 50 yard pitch shot. He stunned everybody however, including Norman, by holing it and thus winning his first and, to date, only Major championship. Of course, Mize got lucky but no one can doubt the technique he showed was anything other than perfect. He gripped down on the club, put the ball back in his stance, kept his hands ahead of the ball through impact and his head still. The ball landed just over the fringe and ran all the way into the hole.

not behind you). This firmness through the ball should help impart a little backspin, helping it to stop quickly on the green.

The most common fault seen with this shot is a deceleration through the ball caused by too long a backswing. The golfer gets to the top of the backswing, instinctively senses the swing is too long and slows down through the ball to prevent the ball from flying over the green. The result is often what the Americans call a 'chili dip', where contact with the ball is so bad it moves only a few inches.

> **REMEMBER**
> Make sure the hands are ahead of the clubface at impact. Don't let your wrists collapse.

20-50 YARDS   THE CHIP AND RUN

If your ball comes to rest just off the green and there are no hazards between it and the hole the wisest shot to play is the chip and run. The ball is lofted over the fringe of the green and then runs the rest of the distance to the hole along the ground. It is safer than the lofted pitch shot from this position because a slightly mishit chip shot will perform much better than a mishit pitch.

> **REMEMBER**
> Your technique for this shot should be similar to that for the pitch shot. The only differences are the choice of club you use and the length of swing.

The set-up
Again, set up with control in mind. Use a 5-iron, 6-iron or 7-iron depending on which club you feel most comfortable with and how much fringe grass you have to clear.

DID YOU KNOW?

The chip and run shot is ideal on links courses such as those found on the coasts of Great Britain and Normandy. These courses rarely have hazards in front of the green, allowing you to play the ball up to the hole along the ground. The turf is usually cropped short and the ground hard which makes the chip and run a far better option than the lofted pitch. In America, however, where the vast majority of courses feature hazards in front of the green and the ground is soft and manicured, the lofted pitch is king. It is so prevalent, in fact, the bump and run has all but disappeared.

Adopt a narrow and open stance with the ball opposite the toe of your back foot so that your hands are in front of the ball. Grip down almost as far as the shaft.

The main problem amateurs have with the set-up is the failure to get comfortable. Relax and press your hands forward slightly so they are ahead of the ball. Don't let your arms, wrists and shoulders tense up by gripping the club too tightly.

The chip and run requires much less wrist action. Keep the hands ahead of the ball at impact and make sure the clubface is still facing the target at the end of the swing.

The swing

The swing is purely an up and down movement of the shoulders with the club moving straight back and straight through. Retain the Y-shape created at address by the clubshaft and your arms throughout the entire swing and simply let the ball get in the way of the clubhead. You will never hit a good shot if you try to help the ball into the air. Don't worry about it, the loft on the clubface is enough to get your ball safely on to the green. Also, if you try to help it up you run the risk of thinning the ball (making contact with the leading edge of the clubface) across the green.

LENGTH OF SHOT DICTATES LENGTH OF BACKSWING

The only difference between your technique for a 10 yard chip and a 20 yard chip is the length of swing. Nothing else should change. Keep the same rhythm and tempo for every shot but simply lengthen your backswing and follow through as the shot gets longer.

THE LOB SHOT

Open the face (above)... ...then grip the club normally (left).

Stand open with the clubface facing the target. Hinge your wrists, keep your head still and drop the club in under the ball.

If a bunker or other obstacle lies between you and the green the chip and run along the ground is far from ideal. The shot facing you may be very short but you have no option but to loft the ball high into the air. It is not a difficult shot to play if the ball is lying on fluffy grass and sitting up. If, however, the ball is lying down in long grass or on hardpan ground the shot becomes a great deal more difficult because it is harder to slide the clubhead underneath the ball. In that situation it may be an idea to cut your losses and chip sideways, avoiding the obstacle altogether.

The set-up
Ideally, you need a lob wedge for this shot. Open your stance a little (feet aiming to the left of the hole) keeping the leading edge of the club square to the hole. Only when you have done this should you grip the club. DO NOT grip the club then open the face. The extra loft will be lost when you come into the ball if you do. Flex your knees more than normal to encourage the clubhead under the ball and play the ball off the instep of your left foot.

The swing
Bring the club back on the line of your feet and let your wrists hinge early. Your head should be still for this shot and your eyes glued to the back of the ball. Make a fullish swing, sliding the club in underneath the ball. The open face will send it up almost vertically.

NB This is a difficult shot to play with a sand wedge, especially off short cropped grass, because of the bounce on the club. Remember, the back of the sole on a sand wedge sits below the leading edge of the clubface (the distance between them known as the bounce) making it difficult to slide the face under the ball. The club has a tendency to hit the ground and bounce up which usually results in you thinning the shot across the green. If, however, your ball is sat up nicely on slightly longer grass then it is possible to play the shot with the sand wedge.

REMEMBER
Use your lob wedge and keep your head stock still.

PITCH SHOT FROM ROUGH

At some courses you'll find the rough encroaches very close to the greens. You may, therefore, find your ball buried in the grass but only 20 feet from the hole.

The set-up
This is a difficult shot as you have to be aggressive enough to get the ball out of the rough but soft enough to prevent it from flying over the green. The secret is to treat it like a greenside bunker shot. Aim your sand wedge at the target but open your stance. Grip down on the club and hold it more firmly to help you cut through the grass without losing control of the clubhead.

Swing with controlled aggression when pitching from the rough and don't be afraid to move some earth.

The swing
The motion is not so much a swing as a shunt. Don't stiffen up, just let the wrists unhinge aggressively through the ball. There is no need for a follow through.

> **REMEMBER**
> Treat the shot like a bunker shot. Be firm and commit yourself to the strike.

PRACTICING YOUR SHORT GAME

Just as hitting range balls into the distance with a driver can become tiresome after a while so hitting chip shot after chip shot can test your patience. Try these five drills to keep short game practice stimulating.

TOWEL UNDER THE ARMS
works on:
Keeping the arms, shoulders and torso 'connected' and working in harmony with each other. Also aids rhythm, which is just as important for short shots as it is full shots. From 50 to 100 yards the various moving parts in your body must work TOGETHER. The wrists must not take over and the arms and shoulders must turn in unison. Flailing arms and 'flicky' wrists will invariably lead to poor contact. This drill succeeds in harmonizing the movements of your body.

how to do it right:
Place a towel under your arms and make short, easy swings with a pitching wedge. Don't allow the towel to drop.

UMBRELLA HOLE
works on:
Pitching accuracy. This is a great drill for those who have trouble with both length and line.

how to do it right:
Simply hit pitch shots with a sand wedge or pitching wedge into an upturned umbrella.

HIT UNDER AN OBSTACLE

works on:
Achieving the correct trajectory for chip and run shots. Too many golfers fail at this shot because they try to help the ball into the air by flicking the right wrist in an attempt to get the club under the ball. You don't really want loft for this shot, however. Ideally the ball should just clear whatever long grass there is between you and the green and then run all the way up to the hole. The natural loft on the club is perfectly sufficient to get the job done.

how to do it right:
Hit chip shots under a bench or something similar. Focus on keeping your hands ahead of the clubhead at address AND IMPACT and keeping the ball low.

STOP THE WRISTS COLLAPSING

works on:
Keeping the left wrist firm through impact. This is another simple yet effective drill to minimize the chances of your wrists collapsing.

how to do it right:
To encourage the wrists to stay firm and therefore the hands to come back to the ball ahead of the clubface, slide a pen or comb in between your left wrist and your glove. This 'stiffens'

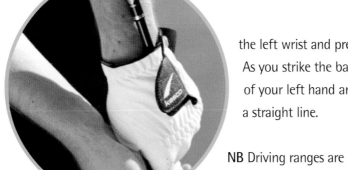

the left wrist and prevents it from hingeing excessively. As you strike the ball the shaft of the club, the back of your left hand and your left arm should now be in a straight line.

NB Driving ranges are normally unsuitable for short game practice. A large field or garden will suffice, however.

OVER YOUR SHOULDER
works on:
Every possible department of your short game. If you miss the green with your approach shot your ball is not always going to find a perfect lie in the rough or fringe. Nor is it consistently going to sit up in a bunker as if you placed it there. Bad lies are going to happen and you have to be prepared for them. This drill, if done regularly, will test not only your technique but your imagination too, taking the fear out of tricky greenside shots. That means you will save your par more often.

how to do it right:
Stand on the green and throw a handful of balls over your shoulder. Play each ball exactly as it lies.

CHAPTER 5

BUNKER PLAY

WHILE MOST PROFESSIONAL players invariably get up and down in two shots from greenside bunkers, most high handicappers will slash about in the sand for several minutes, making little or no progress. It is not overstating the point to say that bunkers put the fear of God into most amateur golfers. The reason for this is a mystery to professionals who find extracating their ball no more difficult than putting it there in the first place. Don't be afraid. With a little knowledge and disciplined practice you can turn the fear into confidence.

THE SIMPLE GREENSIDE BUNKER SHOT

Amateur golfers have two main problems in the sand. Firstly, they don't set up to the ball correctly and secondly they are not certain what is the right amount of sand to take. Some believe if they crash into the sand powerfully they will move so much sand the ball will inevitably be in amongst it somewhere. Others think the best way to play the shot is to pick the ball off the top without moving so much as a grain. Neither method gets consistent results so learn how to play the shot properly.

the set-up

You need to get the ball up quickly so open your stance a little but keep your clubface aiming at the hole. This has the effect of adding loft to the club and forces you to cut across the ball, perfect for this shot. Take up your open stance, place the clubhead behind the ball and **THEN** grip the club. **DO NOT** grip the club then open the face. Play the ball between the instep of your front foot and the centre of your

REMEMBER

Focus on a spot a couple of inches behind the ball, not the ball itself. Hit down on to that spot and scoop the ball out with the right hand feeling dominant. Make a follow through, don't let the club get caught up. ABOVE ALL; Splash, don't crash!!

Ensure that your stance is open but your clubface square to the target. Get settled in the sand.

Don't flick the ball out of the bunker or attempt to smash it out.

stance. Flex your knees almost to the point where you feel you are sitting down and shuffle your feet down into the ground a few inches. These measures help you come into the sand a couple of inches behind the ball and get the clubhead moving underneath it.

Left: The lines show where the club should enter and exit the sand.

Below: A handful of sand is all you need.

Let the club splash in and out of the sand. Make sure you follow through.

the swing

Bring the clubhead away on the line of your feet. Allow your wrists to hinge but don't let your arms and wrists go stiff. Come down aggressively into the sand an inch or two behind the ball and come out of it a few inches in front of where the ball was lying. The right hand should be the dominant force in the swing.

THE PLUGGED LIE

Hit a shot into a bunker shortly after a downpour and your ball is likely to bury itself in the sand (the ball is then said to be 'plugged'). Only the top half of the ball may be visible above the surface. When this happens your sole objective should be to get the ball out of the bunker and anywhere on the green. The shot is simply too difficult for you to

This is a tough shot for any player, but alterations to your set-up will help.

worry about the position of the flag. Even professional players have to bite the bullet in this situation, knowing they have little chance of controlling the ball and getting it to stop close to the hole.

the set-up
Set your body square to the hole but close the clubface a little (delofting it). You need to chop down on the ball hard so play it midway between your feet and grip the club firmly halfway down the handle.

the swing
Aim to come into the sand about an inch behind the ball. Drill the clubhead deep into the sand as hard as you can. You will find it hard to follow through because of the sand's resistance. That's okay, it isn't necessary to follow through this time. The ball will explode out on a cushion of sand with a lot of top spin. So expect the ball to run far more than it would if played from a good lie in the bunker.

Above and right: Come down aggressively and 'explode' the ball out.

FAIRWAY BUNKER SHOT

Those who are new to golf are often terrified of playing out of bunkers. When that bunker is 150 yards or more from the green many players come out in a cold sweat. There really is no need. Again, all it takes to play any bunker shot successfully is a few alterations to your address position. Once they are made you can make a fairly normal swing and the ball should behave as desired.

When taking on this shot be sure the club you are using has sufficient loft to get the ball over the front lip of the bunker. You do not want to strike the ball perfectly only to see it smash into the face of the bunker and dribble back to your feet.

the set-up

If you are to hit your ball 150 yards out of a bunker towards the green you must catch it cleanly, that means removing as little sand as possible. Come into the sand even half an inch behind the ball and the club will meet with such tough resistance that very little power will be transferred into the ball and you'll be lucky to clear the bunker.

In order to catch the ball cleanly just below its equator, you should stand tall and grip a couple of inches down the handle.

Grip down and play the ball back in your stance. Keep your swing short and your lower body still.

Also, don't shuffle your feet down into the sand as you would for greenside bunker shots where you are trying to hit the sand before the ball. Try to remain 'on the surface'. Play the ball an inch further back in your stance than normal (towards the centre) to help guarantee you catch the ball, not the sand, first.

the swing

As you are about to take the club back imagine the ball is lying on a sheet of thin ice, or concrete. This will certainly encourage you to pick it cleanly off the top without disturbing too much sand. Keep the swing short and quiet – that means a smooth takeaway and no lunges from the top of the backswing – and pick the ball off the top.

REMEMBER
Pick the ball cleanly off the top trying to disturb as little sand as possible.

The less sand you take, the further the ball will travel.

PRACTICING BUNKER PLAY

TRY DIFFERENT CLUBS AND DIFFERENT LIES IN THE SAND

works on: Enhancing your feel and developing your imagination. It would be terribly misleading to suggest there are no fundamental rules when it comes to bunker play, but great feel and imagination are really what separate the greats from the merely efficients. To develop a great short game you have to be willing to experiment and become familiar with how the ball reacts from different lies.

how to do it right:
Don't rely solely on your sand wedge out of sand. Practice hitting shots with a pitching wedge and even a 9-iron. And don't just hit balls that are sat up nicely. Try a few from plugged, downhill, uphill and sidehill lies too. As with everything in golf, practice makes perfect.

DID YOU KNOW?
South African legend, Gary Player, who is recognized as being the best bunker player in the history of the game, practices his sand play so much he has ground down the grooves of at least six sand wedges during his career.

THE GREATEST BUNKER SHOT EVER?

A year after Larry Mize's dramatic chip in at Augusta, Scotland's Sandy Lyle came to the 18th in the final round needing a birdie three to win. He virtually destroyed his chances of doing that, however, when he hit his drive into one of the two massive fairways bunkers that guard the left hand side of the fairway. He was faced with an uphill shot of 150 yards from sand, never an easy prospect and a million times harder when you know you have to pull it off to win The Masters. Fortunately, he had a good lie and the lip was low enough for him to take a 7-iron. He hit the ball clean as a whistle. Not only did he clear the lip he made it all the way to the green as well, the ball spinning back to within 15ft of the hole. Lyle picked the ball so cleanly off the surface he disturbed only a few grains of sand. Considering the amount of pressure he was under, it was surely one of the greatest shots ever hit. He holed the putt and became the first British golfer to win The Masters.

CHAPTER 6

PUTTING

QUITE SIMPLY, a good putter is a match for anyone. There is nothing that will boost your confidence, and destroy your opponent's, quicker than a succession of holed putts. Good putting can turn a potentially disastrous score into an acceptable one or totally break the spirit of your matchplay opponent.

In a typical round almost half the total number of shots you play will be with the putter. It makes a lot of sense, therefore, to use one with which you feel comfortable. Take time when picking your putter. Don't simply plump for the brand your favourite player uses. It may feel good to him but totally alien to you. Try as many as you can. If the one you prefer the most happens to be the cheapest or ugliest buy it anyway. It's no good having a putter that costs £200 if you don't feel confident with it.

Putting is a very individualistic discipline. Watch five different players and it's likely you'll see five very different methods. Some, like Jack Nicklaus or Colin Montgomerie, tend to crouch, bending over at the waist quite considerably. Others, like Ben Crenshaw and Brad Faxon, stand taller. Some players favour short putters which allow them to hang their arms naturally while others swear by 4ft long broomhandle putters. Obviously, you need to develop a method that feels right to you. Don't worry if you look totally different to the guy next to you on the practice putting green. If you're the one holing all the putts he's the one that should be worried. But while there is a lot of room for individual experimentation when putting, there are one or two fundamentals that every golfer should remember.

THE GRIP

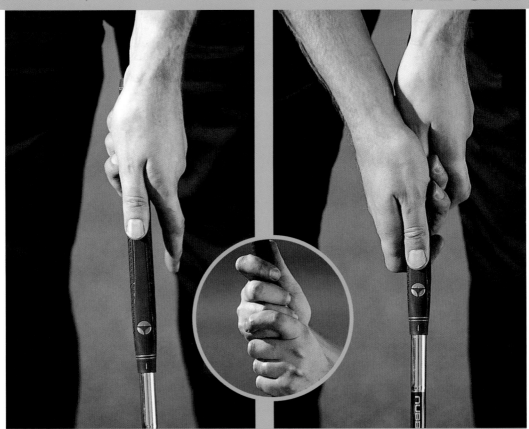

The reverse overlap grip, as used by the majority of professional and low handicap golfers. Note how the index finger of the top hand sits on top of the fingers of the bottom hand (inset).

There are no hard and fast rules determining how you should hold the putter. Bernhard Langer has invented a number of unconventional putting grips to combat the yips during his career and has been very successful with most of them. Whether you use one of Langer's grips or develop one of your own is entirely up to you. Whichever grip you do decide to use, however, make sure that:

1) the back of your left hand and the palm of you right hand are facing the target thus forming a neutral grip.

2) you hold the club lightly.

REVERSE OVERLAP
The most common type of putting grip is called the 'reverse overlap' (see opposite). It is popular because it brings the hands together as one unit on the grip in a comfortable and unfussy way. The putting stroke is predominantly an up and down movement of the shoulders, the hands play very little part other than to hold the club. It is beneficial, therefore, to bring the hands together rather than set them apart which encourages them to become too active and override the motion of the shoulders.

The reverse overlap is basically the same as the Vardon grip you might use for your long game, the only major difference being the positions of the left index finger and the little finger of the right hand (see inset). Instead of the little finger of the right hand riding piggy back on the index finger of the left hand the roles are reversed so that the index finger moves out on top of the fingers of the right hand and the little finger is back in contact with the grip. Both thumbs sit centrally on top of the grip.

Play around with it until it feels comfortable always ensuring, however, the palms of your hands are pretty much facing each other and that your grip is light, but never loose.

Again, don't worry if your grip isn't identical to the one shown. As long as it follows the two main criteria mentioned above you should have a sound grip.

CACK-HANDED
When Langer first suffered with the yips he adopted this method where the hands are reversed. Other pros such as Nick Faldo have experimented with this grip and Irish golfer Padraig Harrington has used it virtually his entire career. Its merit lies in the levelling of the shoulders at address which promotes a true pendulum stroke. Notice how the back of the left hand and the palm of the right still face the target.

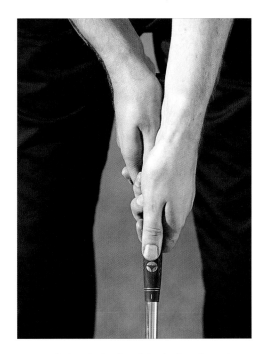

The cack-handed grip might look awkward but it is popular with many good players.

THE GRIP WITH NO NAME

After going through another cruel bout of the yips in the early nineties Langer came up with this. It never quite caught on as much as the cack-handed technique but it served Langer very well. The inside of the left forearm is held tight against the shaft and handle of the putter by the right hand. This effectively takes the hands out of the stroke altogether allowing you to rely solely on the more predictable and manageable motion of the shoulders.

REMEMBER
Your grip on the putter must be light so your forearms are free of tension. The palms of your hands should face each other.

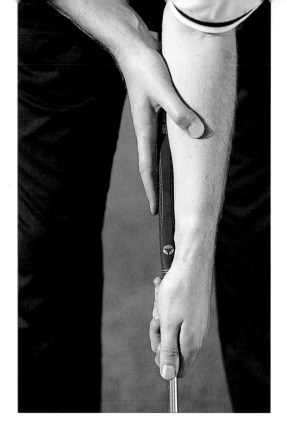

Top German golfer, Bernhard Langer and Australian Rodger Davis both found success with this odd looking grip.

STANCE AND POSTURE

Stand tall and relax the shoulders. Hunched (middle) and stooped (right) address positions will never promote a smooth, repeating stroke.

You became aware in chapter 2 of the importance of comfort and balance when setting up for a full shot and the same applies when putting. Comfort is paramount and you must stand to the ball in a way that lets your head and centre of gravity remain stock still throughout the stroke.

The position is not dissimilar to the set-up for a full shot. The knees are flexed a little and the body is bent over at the waist. Your feet should be about shoulder

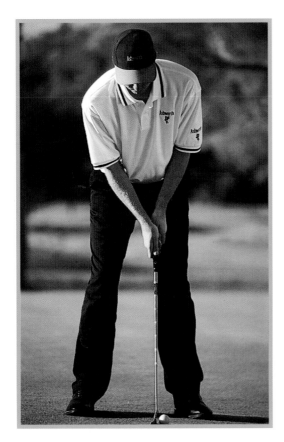

Left: Play the ball just inside your left instep.

width apart, or maybe a little closer together. Try to make your set-up as orthodox as possible, as this will certainly promote a smoother, more repetitive putting stroke, but again, allow for a little individual interpretation.

BALL POSITION
Jack Nicklaus positions his head well behind the ball when putting to enable him to look down the line of the putt. Justin Leonard, the 1997 British Open Champion, positions his ball quite a distance from his body so that he almost has

to reach for it. Both are great putters which proves that as long as you're comfortable with the position of the ball and you play it from the same place in relation to your stance every time, you can have it pretty much where you like. Remember this, however; no one ever became a good putter by playing the ball nearer the back foot than the front and no great putter ever positioned his ball so close to his feet that a vertical line down from his eyes hit the ground outside the ball.

The best spot to position the ball in order to guarantee solid, square contact most often is directly beneath your eyes. Find out where this is by dropping a ball from the bridge of your nose on to the ground. Tiger Woods is a fan of this particular drill and it hasn't done him any harm.

Your eyes should ideally be positioned directly over the ball.

REMEMBER
Comfort is again essential to your address position.

THE BASIC PUTTING STROKE

If there was one word that best described how your putting stroke should feel it would be pendulum. It should be smooth, unhurried and accelerate through the ball.

The movement of the clubhead comes from the rocking of the shoulders. The arms, hands and wrists should not be absolutely rigid, as this would result in a loss of feel, but they must not be the engine room of the stroke either. No part of the body, other than the shoulders, arms and hands must move. There is no shifting of the weight and your head must remain absolutely still with your eyes trained on the back of the ball. To ensure there is no movement in the hips and legs feel that your knees stay in exactly the same position throughout the stroke. Above all stay relaxed and focus on the up and down motion – rather than a twisting motion — of the left shoulder.

> **REMEMBER**
>
> Keep it smooth, slowly back and slowly through. Tempo is as important to your putting as it is for your long game.

Keep your knees and your head still and accelerate the putterhead through impact.

TEMPO

This is as important on the greens as it is on the tee. Your stroke must be smooth and free of any jerky movements. Only with good tempo can you hope to make solid contact with the ball with a square clubface. Thinking 'one-two' ('one' on the backswing, 'two' on the through swing) as you swing the putter is a good way to develop tempo but you can devise your own method. One way of promoting a smooth takeaway is to hover the putterhead above the ground as you address the ball (right). This prevents the putterhead from getting 'stuck' as the hands come back. Make sure you use the same method every time you putt.

THOSE TESTING THREE-FOOTERS

Focusing on hitting the back of the hole will encourage a bold and confident stroke.

The list of promising careers that have been cut short by a failure to hole out confidently from three or four feet is considerable. Fred Couples has often had a problem with this length putt evidenced by his short, sharp stroke. And Langer, of course, has been tormented from this range at various times in his career.

Part of the problem is that everyone expects you to hole it. You begin to fear what the reaction of your playing partners might be should you miss and that takes your concentration away from the job at hand. Also, three or four foot putts can have some break in them (sideways movement caused by a slope) and a strong breeze will certainly affect the path the ball takes too. That can make some short putts anything but straightforward.

The secret is to be bold, take the break out of the putt and aim straight for the hole. You may miss some by being too bold but you will definitely hole more than you miss as the temptation to second-guess yourself over the line of the putt, usually a fatal error, will be removed. Another good tip is to focus on hitting the back of the cup. Don't try to dribble the ball over the front edge as this will let any break in the putt take hold of your ball and push it to the side of the hole. Apart from that, use your normal positive, pendulum stroke.

THE LAG PUTT FROM 40 FEET

Your task from this distance is to get down in no more than two shots. You can't realistically hope to hole a putt of this length but you can avoid an ugly three-putt every time. A very effective way to ensure you get down in no more than two is to imagine the hole is the size of a dustbin lid. Creating this bigger target in your mind immediately takes some of the pressure off you and allows you to make a smooth stroke with your normal

Imagine the hole is the size of a dustbin lid. You will feel more relaxed over the putt.

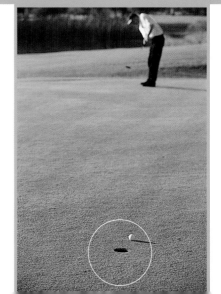

tempo. Once you get your ball inside the dustbin lid the second putt should be easy. Good tempo is crucial on putts this long. Continue to use the 'one-two' method (or whatever words you use) but make the stroke longer. If you watched the same pro golfer for 18 holes you would notice his tempo for every single putt, be it four feet or 40 feet, is the same. The only thing that changes is the length of the stroke.

NICE PUTT, SHAME ABOUT THE CHIP

When Costantino Rocca came to the 72nd hole of the 1995 Open Championship at St Andrews he needed a birdie three to get into a play-off with American, John Daly. He hit a long straight drive but then his nerves got the better of him and he totally duffed the chip shot. The divot flew further than the ball which dribbled pathetically into the Valley of Sin, leaving him a mammoth 60 foot putt. The putt was not only long but at the mercy of a steep incline as well which made judging the pace particularly difficult. Rocca couldn't have judged the pace any better, however. His ball never wavered on its journey into the hole and the crowd went berserk as Rocca fell to his knees in disbelief. It was perhaps, the greatest ever putt in the history of the British Open.

EVERY PUTT IS STRAIGHT

How to read the break in a putt is something you will learn only with experience. Don't expect to arrive on your first green and hole a 20ft putt with six feet of break. It won't come that quickly. Holing putts with borrow (another word for break) is, of course, not just about picking the right line. The speed at which the ball travels affects how the ball reacts to the slope. The harder you hit the ball the straighter it will travel. Hit the ball softly and the break will take a more immediate affect, causing the ball to fall away on the low side of the hole. Over time you will develop a 'sixth sense' which will enable you to combine the correct line with the correct pace for the putt.

Align your putterface and body with the apex of the break, (shown here by the tee).

You will get a much better idea of potential breaks and the speed of the putt if you look at it from all angles. Take the shade of the grass into account when thinking about the speed of a putt.

There is one invaluable tip that will make sloping putts seem less problematic however; treat every putt as though it were straight. Study the putt and decide where the ball will break the most. Then imagine this point, the apex of the break, is the hole and that a ball travelling towards it will move in a straight line. Align yourself (putterface and body) with your new target. All you have to do now is get a feel for the pace of the putt.

READING THE GREEN: Study your putt from behind the ball, behind the hole and from the sides. This will help give you a clear picture in your mind of how the ball will break and at what speed you should hit the putt.

ALSO WORTH NOTING: The darker the green and the longer the grass is, the slower the putt will be and the straighter it will run. Grass tends to grow towards the nearest water so bear in mind the whereabouts of any water features when lining up a putt. Greens are mown in strips. If the grass is growing towards you, (dark strips) your putt will be slower than if the grass is growing away from you (light strips).

SUMMARY OF PUTTING

Putting is easy. Really, how difficult can it be to roll a ball along the ground into a hole with a stick designed for that very purpose? We make it difficult by becoming over technical and treating what is in reality a very simple exercise as though it were very demanding. Keep it simple and remember three main lessons:

1) the stroke is a pendulum motion.

2) treat every putt as though it were straight.

3) your head must remain absolutely still.

PRACTICING YOUR PUTTING

Below are four drills to prevent practicing this department of the game from becoming dull.

PUTT ONE-HANDED

works on:
Smoothness of stroke, increasing your control of the putterhead and the acceleration of the putter through the ball.

how to do it right:
Very simply putt with only your right hand. Place your other hand behind your back. Hit 10 putts with one hand from five feet then revert to using both hands trying to recreate the sensation of putting with one hand.

BALL MARKER UNDER THE BALL

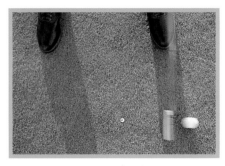

works on:
Keeping your head still. So many putts are missed by players looking up to see where their ball has gone. They hope to watch the ball disappear rather than listen to it drop. In doing so they risk affecting the path of the putterhead and the quality of strike.

how to do it right:
Place your ball on top of a ball marker or similar flat object and make a normal stroke. As the ball moves away from the ball marker your eyes should still be focusing on it rather than the ball. It is a good idea to combine this drill with all the others so that you are constantly working on keeping your head still.

TWO-PUTTER RAILWAY TRACK

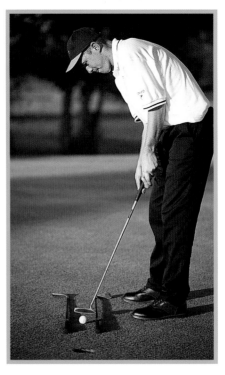

works on:
Maintaining a 'square to square' putterhead through the ball on short putts.
For these putts, the putterhead should ideally move straight back and straight through, remaining square to the line of the putt at all times (as the putt gets

longer so the putterhead starts to move on more of a curve, coming back slightly inside the target line).

how to do it right:
Put two clubs on the ground slightly more than a putterhead's width apart. They must run parallel to each other and run towards the hole. As you make your stroke keep the putterhead inside the two clubs for the entire stroke. Do this at least 50 times to groove that straight back and straight through movement.

PUTT TO DIFFERENT DISTANCES
works on:
Enhancing your feel for distance. It is a fact that most golfers have more trouble getting the pace of a putt right than the line. If you've played golf before you will know that getting the ball to roll in the general direction of the hole is not that difficult whereas achieving the right distance from long range can sometimes be tricky.

how to get it right:
Stick four tee-pegs in the ground, 10ft, 20ft, 30ft and 40ft away. Then hit balls to them at random; e.g. two to 20ft, three to 10ft, one to 40ft etc. Do this for at least 20 minutes to build your confidence.

TROUBLE SHOTS

WHAT A DULL OLD GAME golf would be if every hole was flat and every shot you hit, straight. Rest assured, there will be times when you need to curve the ball left or right round trees, hit a high shot over an over-hanging branch or a low one under the wind. Then there will be times you have to play the ball from below your feet or hit it off an uphill slope. Actually, the instances when you are faced with a perfectly flat, straight shot could be very rare indeed. Knowing how best to deal with these tricky situations when they arise — and they will — is therefore an essential part of your development.

SHAPING THE BALL

Beginners look on amazed when the world's great golfers intentionally curve the ball to the left or right in order to avoid trees and various other hazards. They assume the pros are blessed with the ability to perform magic and that the shots the pros hit require a level of skill they could never hope to attain. But hitting finesse shots such as a draw or fade is not as difficult as it may first appear. In fact, all you have to do to hit them successfully is alter how you stand to the ball slightly then swing the club in much the same way you would for any other shot.

HITTING A DRAW

A draw is a shot that curves gently from right to left and imparts top spin on the ball thus making it run a few extra yards. Because of the extra distance you get with a draw it is a useful shot to have up your sleeve on long holes.

The set-up To curve the ball from right to left your clubface must be closed in relation to your body when you hit the ball. To pre-program this into your swing start, as you would on all shots, by aiming your clubface where you want the ball to land. Then aim your body (feet, knees, hips, shoulders) to the right of your target on the line you want the ball to start.

That really is all you have to do but if you want to further ensure the clubface is closed when you make contact with the ball strengthen your grip a touch by moving your bottom hand under the grip a little more.

Aim your body where you want the ball to start (right of your target) but the clubface where you want the ball to finish.

The swing
Just make your normal, smooth swing ensuring you stay behind the ball through impact.

REMEMBER
Stay behind the ball all the way through impact and allow the clubhead to release.

The draw is pre-programmed into your set-up, so then it's just a case of making your normal swing.

SHOT OF THE YEAR

Sergio Garcia's second shot to the 16th hole in the final round of the 1999 USPGA championship was a shot only someone of his unprecedented nerve and skill could possibly hope to pull off. His drive at this tough dogleg par 4 ran out of fairway, the ball coming to rest tight against a tree. The tree all but cut off his line to the green and the ball was nestled nastily in between a couple of pertruding roots. To have any chance of finding the putting surface he would have to loft the ball over the roots, starting it way to the left to avoid the tree and put a tremendous amount of cut spin (left to right) on the ball to get it curving back towards the target. The American commentators who were calling the action at the time couldn't believe he was taking the shot on but, miraculously, he not only made a good connection but put enough slice on the ball to bring it back to the green as well. He ran after it like a young Seve Ballesteros and a new star was born.

HITTING A FADE

A fade curves gently from left to right and flies higher than a draw. It has cut spin which brings the ball to a halt more quickly than draw spin. It is, therefore, an ideal shot to hit into the green.

The set-up
Aim the clubface at the target, as always, but this time aim your body slightly to the left of it, as shown. This opens your clubface to the line of your body which

should ensure the clubface is open when you make contact – thus putting cut spin on the ball. But to guarantee it is, weaken your grip by moving your right hand over the top of the grip when you set-up to the ball.

The swing
The open face has been pre-programmed so there is nothing you have to do to further encourage the left to right spin.

REMEMBER
Aim the clubface at the target but your body to the left. Hold off the release of the club a little.

Left: Make the swing and watch it curve.

HITTING A HIGH SHOT

If you find yourself behind a tree your only option may be to go over it. But the club you need to get over the tree may not give you sufficient distance to get you to the green. In this situation you have to take enough club to get the ball to the green and alter your set-up in such a way that puts a few degrees more loft on the clubface and encourages an upward strike through the ball.

The set-up
Play the ball further forward than normal, off the toes of the front foot is about right, and open your stance slightly.

The swing
Make your normal swing but have the feeling you are sliding the clubface under the ball, sending it high. Chase after the ball by throwing the hands and clubhead up high as you follow through.

REMEMBER
Stay behind the ball. Slide the club in underneath the ball and hoist it high.

Top: Play the ball forward in your stance, opposite you left big toe.
Above: Make a full follow through and finish 'high'.

Left: The ball will set off on a steep trajectory.

HITTING A LOW SHOT

The ability to keep the ball low under the wind is a valuable shot to have in your repertoire, especially if you are playing a seaside course in Great Britain or Northern Europe. It's also a pretty useful shot if you are forced to punch one under an over-hanging branch.

The set-up
For this shot you obviously need to deloft the clubface. So play it further back in your stance, towards your back foot. Your hands should now be well in front of the clubface. Also grip down the club an inch or two. These amendments will give you a sense of stability and control.

The swing
The wind will play havoc with the clubhead if you go all the way back and all the way through. So shorten your backswing and curtail the follow through to give you a better chance of making a firm, balanced punch through the ball. Your hands must be well ahead of the ball as you reach impact if you are to maintain the reduced loft on the club that you created at address. After impact try not to release the clubhead as you would on a normal shot. Keep the wrists firm through the ball.

Top: Position the ball off your back foot. Your hands should be well ahead of the ball at address. Feet together.

Above and left: Keep your swing short and aggressive, 'punching' through the ball with your right hand dominant.

If you are trying to keep the ball under the wind you must not come down too aggressively or the ball is likely to balloon up into the wind and get blown way off course. Swing smoothly through the ball, remembering to keep your hands well ahead of the ball at impact.

> **REMEMBER**
> Your hands must be well ahead of the clubface at impact. Punch down and through the ball. Don't try to hit the ball too hard, just maintain your normal smooth rhythm.

TROUBLESOME LIES

UPHILL LIE

Take an extra club, feel your weight on the back foot and sweep the ball towards the target.

The set-up Because you are hitting off an uphill slope loft is effectively added to the clubface so you will need to take one more club (a 6-iron is 'one more club' than a 7-iron) than the yardage suggests. As you stand to the ball, drop your right shoulder, letting the majority of your weight shift naturally on to your back foot, and so that your spine is again perpendicular to the ground. This tilting of the upper body towards your back foot helps you simulate a shot off a flat lie, preventing you from digging the club deep into the ground before you make contact with the ball.

The swing Keep it short and firm. Take the club back too far and you will find it very difficult to maintain your balance. Your legs need to be stable so keep them fairly quiet. The upper body should dominate the swing. As you approach impact feel that you are going to sweep the ball off the turf without taking much of a divot.

DOWNHILL LIE

The set-up

Just do the opposite to the uphill lie. Take one less club than the yardage suggests because the slope effectively takes loft off the clubface and the ball is liable to run more. Then drop your left shoulder and position the majority of your weight on your front foot (as shown). Your spine should now be perpendicular to the slope. Play the ball an inch or two further back in your stance than you would for a similar length shot off flat ground. This will enable you to strike the ball as the club reaches the bottom of the swing. The ball will fade naturally so aim slightly to the left of your target.

The swing

It is relatively difficult to achieve solid contact from this lie. You need to slow the swing down and maintain your rhythm perhaps more consciously than at any other time. Pick the club up quite steeply and drop it in behind the ball, staying down all the way through the hitting area. Feel that your hands move on down the slope after impact. Do not bring them up sharply.

Play the ball back in your stance and keep the weight forward through impact.

BALL BELOW FEET

The set-up Because the ball is, in effect, slightly further away from you than it would be if the ground were flat you need to hold the club right at the top of the grip. Then, because the slope will naturally force you to fall forwards you need to feel that most of the weight is placed on your heels. Bend your knees a little more than is usual and stick your rear end out to help you maintain the weight on your heels. The lie of the land will cause the ball to curve to the right so aim a little left of your target.

The swing You will feel your swing has to be quite upright if you are to deliver the clubhead with the sole as flat on the ground as possible, and you should go with what the slope dictates. As with all shots off sloping lies you should concentrate on rhythm, as any jerky movements will cause you to lose your balance.

Right: Push your weight back on your heels and hold the club at the top of the grip.

Aim a little left of the target as the ball is likely to fade to the right.

BALL ABOVE FEET

The set-up
The ball is a little closer to you this time so you have to grip down the club to have a chance of keeping the sole flat on the ground. Stand a little taller than you would if the ball was below your feet to guard against the club driving straight down into the ground.

Your swing will inevitably be a little more around your body, not up and down. This will encourage the ball to curve from right to left in the air. Bear this is mind for your set-up.

The swing
The changes you have made to your set-up allow you to make a normal swing. Don't fight the slope which will force you to swing more around your body. To be sure of making good contact keep the swing short and sweet, as you would for all potential trouble shots like this one.

Left: Push your weight on to your toes and grip down the club.

REMEMBER
To hit these shots successfully all you need do is make a couple of alterations to your set-up. The swing should then be as normal and natural as you can make it.

Swing smoothly so as not to lose your balance.

BALL IN A DIVOT

Because of the ignorant few who fail to replace their divots it is more than likely you will, in the course of your round, have to play at least one shot from a two-inch deep hole in the ground.

Not everyone replaces their divots as they should do, so be prepared for this.

The set-up
The set up for this shot is very similar to that for a low, punchy shot. You have to come down steeply into the ball because it is sat down under the surface of the ground. With that in mind, you should play the ball back in your stance which will push your hands ahead of the ball. Grip down the club a little as well to give you a better sense of control. To aid the steep attack into the ball push a little more weight on to your front foot at address.

The swing
Swing with controlled aggression. That means you must come down hard into the ball but maintain your balance and tempo at the same time. Your hands must be ahead of the ball as you hit it. It is inevitable you will take a fairly substantial divot – larger than the one you found yourself in to begin with. Keep your wrists firm as you plough through the ball.

Come down hard and drive through the ball.

TAKING IT TO THE COURSE

HAVING A SOLID and reliable golf swing is one of the most important factors in becoming a better golfer. But will it guarantee you will shoot low scores on the course? I'm afraid not. There have been many professionals over the years that have had aesthetically beautiful swings but have been unable to make the grade. Clearly then there are other factors, such as fitness and mental toughness, which make up the complete golfer – elements which you need to add to your game.

NOBILIS
1 PAR 4
S.I. 2

430
398
336

PUTTING IT INTO PRACTICE

David Duval, Justin Leonard and Jim Furyk are all among the world's top 20 golfers. They rarely fail to break 70 and have won countless millions of dollars between them. And yet their golf swings are radically unconventional, some would even say ugly. How can that happen? How does a golfer with as seemingly flawed a swing as Furyk shoot such good scores, on such difficult courses?

Clearly, the way a player swings the golf club is only a very small part of the equation. Other factors such as confidence, physical fitness, putting and course management (the way you conduct yourself on the course and the shot-related decisions you make) play as big a role, if not bigger, in determining your level of success. The aim of this chapter is to show you how to achieve your best possible results without becoming bogged down with swing thoughts.

PREPARING FOR THE ROUND

Every golfer, professionals and amateurs alike, should ensure they have everything they are likely to need during the round packed in their bag before they arrive at the 1st tee. Check to see you have all 14 clubs, enough balls and tees, a pitch mark repairer, pencil and ball marker. Pack the rain gear and umbrella if the weather looks at all dubious and gouge out the mud from the soles of your golf shoes. Put a banana or two in your bag and a bottle of water to keep your energy high and prevent dehydration. Put in another sweater, a bobble hat and maybe some gloves if you think it could turn cold. In short, be prepared!

Make sure you have packed everything you will need before taking to the course.

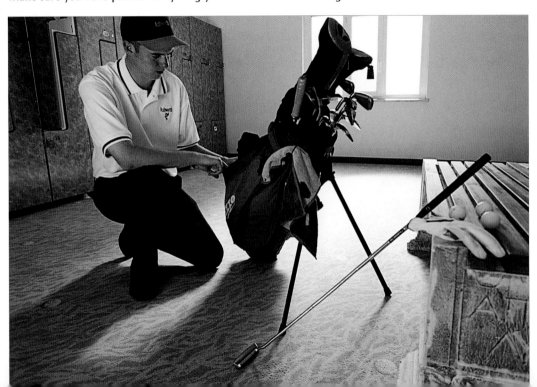

THE PRO'S WARM-UP ROUTINE

If you've ever been to a professional tournament to watch your favourite players in action you will probably have observed how they warm up for the round. Without exception they will arrive at the range at least an hour before they are due to tee off and spend the

time attuning themselves physically and mentally for the task ahead. This usually involves hitting about 10 balls with each of the even-numbered irons and the driver (starting with the shortest and working down), stroking a few easy putts to groove their stroke, and 20 minutes or so of chipping and bunker play. It is important to realize the time is definitely not spent practicing (this is not a good time to start worrying about technique), but warming the muscles up, building a rhythm for the day and playing the course in the mind before arriving on the 1st tee. There is no mad rush for the tee and no risk of causing themselves an injury.

Above and left: A professional golfer's day starts with an hour's warm-up on the practice range. He will hit a few balls with every club focusing solely on developing a good rhythm.

If you are rushed, a few stretches and short game practice will prevent any pulled muscles and help you develop a good feel for shots around the greens. Finish by swinging two clubs simultaneously.

HOW TO SPEND 10 MINUTES IF YOU'RE RUSHED

Professional golfers have to prepare themselves in such a way as to ensure they start performing to their potential right from the start. Golf is how they earn their living so it's no good them arriving on the 1st tee cold and eventually finding their rhythm on the 5th or 6th hole. You would do well to copy their thorough warm-up session, of course, but your hectic and demanding schedule away from the golf club probably won't allow it. So how do you warm-up for a round, prevent yourself from pulling any muscles and arrive on the 1st tee undaunted by the prospect of having to slide one between the fairway bunkers if you've only got 10 minutes in which to do it?

You must start with a few stretches. Place a club across your shoulders and turn it as far as it will go before you start to feel the strain. Don't overdo it, now is not a good time to break your spine. After two or three minutes of that head for the putting green. Hit 10 uphill three-footers. They should be uphill because you want to be aggressive through the ball, grooving a confident stroke and three feet from the hole because holing putts works wonders for your confidence. Hit a few chip shots on to the practice chipping green if there is one, or near the putting green if there isn't (you probably won't be permitted to hit chip shots on to the practice putting green). Finish by swinging two clubs simultaneously. This is a good way to free up your muscles and establish a slow, smooth rhythm. Spend a little time looking down the 1st hole,

imagining yourself splitting the fairway with your drive. This will help settle a few nerves. When you come to hit your tee-shot try to recreate the same rhythm you established when swinging the two clubs together and commit yourself fully to the shot.

> **REMEMBER**
>
> A full hour's warm up is ideal but five minutes is infinitely better than none at all. Stretch some muscles and do what you can to develop a comfortable rhythm if you are pushed for time.

PREPARING FOR A SHOT

THE PRE-SHOT ROUTINE
How you spend the 30 seconds or so before you actually commence your swing has a major influence on the outcome of the shot. All good players, and I mean ALL, spend that time going through what is known as a pre-shot routine. A typical pre-shot routine will usually involve standing a few yards behind the ball to visualize the shot you want to play, moving up to the side of the ball, placing the clubhead behind it and then settling into a comfortable address position. The actual elements of the routine are not important – you can approach the ball however you want. What is hugely important, however, is that whatever you do you follow the same procedure, for every single shot. The aim is to make it such a habit you do it without thinking. That way you will build a repetitive rhythm that will last from the moment you take the club out of the bag right through to the finish of the swing. Concentrating on what

It is essential you develop a pre-shot routine. Visualize the shot, aim the clubface, aim the body and settle into your address position.

you are trying to achieve with the shot while
you progress through your pre-shot routine
will also help you eliminate technical swing
thoughts, which prevent you from swinging
the club with any rhythm.

COURSE MANAGEMENT

The ability to play the right shot at the right time and plot his way round the course is what
made Jack Nicklaus the most successful golfer ever. Several golfers of his generation could boast
more stylish swings but not one of them could hold a candle to him when it came to avoiding
potential disaster and positioning the ball in a spot to make the next shot easier. Golf was almost
like a game of chess to him. A battle of wits rather than brute strength.

If you want to shoot better scores without changing your swing, improving your course
management is the way to do it. I'm not suggesting you analyze the shot you're faced with to
the same degree that Nicklaus did – your head would probably start to hurt after a while if you

did – but there are a few factors you
should take into account every time you
prepare to fire.

DISTANCE

If you have a course
planner/yardage chart take a little time
to calculate the yardage to the hole and
to any hazards that lurk near your
intended target. You should know
roughly how far you hit each club and
knowing you have the right club in your
hand will do wonders for your
confidence. Make sure the club you take
is enough to get you over any hazards
short of your target. Putting from the
back of the green is better than having
to play out of a bunker or drop out of a
lake in front of it. Also, if there is a

Do not take on a shot in competition you
haven't hit successfully a few times in
practice. Consult your yardage planner to
discover the exact distance to the target.

pond, stream or bunker just in front of the green which you don't believe you can clear, don't assume that getting as close to the hazard with your layup shot is the wisest move. If you're more confident of getting your ball close to the hole with your next shot from 100 yards than you are from 70, then hit your layup shot to 100 yards.

PLAY AWAY FROM TROUBLE

DID YOU KNOW?
When Ben Hogan won the British Open at Carnoustie in 1953 he stuck rigidly to the game plan he had devised before the Championship started. So rigidly did he adhere to it throughout the tournament, in fact, it was rumoured he hit his drives into the divots he had created during the previous round.

It sounds obvious, but don't court disaster by hitting towards hazards. At this early stage in your golfing career you would be wise to keep the ball in play at all costs even if that means playing ultra safe by hitting a short iron further up the fairway rather than going for the green with a long iron. Always look for a safe bail out area, where you can hit your ball to without fear of it falling into a water hazard or pot bunker. If there is even the smallest doubt in your mind that you are not striking the ball well enough to clear the lake or bunker in front of the green, play up short or to the side of it and go for the green with your next shot.

Aiming for the left side of the fairway, in this example, will result in a longer second shot but you will avoid the water down the right.

LEAVE YOURSELF AN UPHILL PUTT

The more you play the more you will discover uphill putts are easier to make than those that travel downhill. That's because you instinctively make a smoother, more confident stroke through the ball if the putt is uphill. On downhill putts many people have a tendency to decelerate through the ball, fearing it will finish well past the hole if they miss. With that in mind always try to leave your approach shot to the green under the hole, thus leaving yourself an uphill putt.

The pros try to do this with all their full approach shots but although this will be beyond your capabilities, you can always try to do it with your chip shots.

Always aim to leave yourself an uphill putt.

PLAYING WITH WHAT YOU'VE GOT

Experimenting with your swing in the course of a round is asking for trouble. You should learn to play with what you've got. If you arrive on the 16th tee and you've hit 15 slices in a row the chances are you're going to hit another one. Tee your ball up on the left hand side of the teeing ground and aim down the left hand side of the fairway. That way, if you do hit the ball straight it will finish in the left side of the fairway but if you continue to do what you've done all day, and slice the ball, it should finish in the middle or right side of the fairway. Similarly, if you're consistently hooking the ball tee it up on the right side of the teeing ground and aim down the right side of the fairway.

Tee up on the left if you are consistently slicing the ball...and on the right if you are fighting a hook.

BE REALISTIC

If you're new to the game it is highly unlikely you are going to be able to pull off miracle shots like threading your ball through a narrow gap between two trees 20 yards ahead of you. Your sole objective in cases like these must be to get the ball back in

the fairway from where you can attack the green, even if that means coming out sideways. There is absolutely nothing to be gained from trying to smash a 3-wood out of the forest, hitting a tree and having the ball ricochet around before falling at your feet. Always err on the side of caution when you find yourself in this type of situation. Look for the safest route out of trouble.

REMEMBER

A little thought goes a long way and can help prevent the really big numbers from going down on your scorecard. Always bear in mind a drive that travels 200 yards down the middle of the fairway is infinitely better positioned than a drive that travels 280 yards into a lake.

Above and left: A 3-wood from here? Don't be stupid. Play out sideways into safety with a short iron.

NEVER GIVE UP
Start your round
with a string of double bogies and you're
probably going to feel a little down on
yourself. That's natural, but try not to stay
down for long. Always remember you have
a handicap that allows you some bad holes.
Discipline yourself to get back on track and
you'll feel a whole lot better than you
would if you spent the rest of the round
cursing your equipment. Remember where
you are: on a beautiful golf course on a
glorious day. So life ain't so bad.

**Bad start? Don't give up, you have still got
several holes to turn your score around.**

THE MENTAL SIDE

It's true of any sport, and golf in particular, that what goes on inside your head has an
immeasurable impact on how well you perform. Indeed, there are those who could
probably convince you your thought processes have a much more significant impact on
your golf score than your technique. That may or may not be true but what is irrefutable is
that the confident golfer beats the negative golfer 99 times out of 100. It would be
possible to write several weighty books on the psychological side of the game but because
space is limited here you will find just four mental techniques that I believe will help your
game profoundly, without you having to make a single alteration to your swing.

SET YOURSELF GOALS
It has been scientifically proven that goal setters
improve quicker than those that simply turn up and hit off without giving much thought to
what they are hoping to achieve. So get in the habit, at the start of every season, month and
round, of setting yourself *realistic* targets. That certainly does not mean giving yourself the
task of routinely breaking 70 by the end of the year if you are having trouble breaking 100 in
January. Do that and you are very likely to be disappointed come December 31st if the lowest
score you managed all year was 86. You'll probably be inclined to feel you're not improving at
all and end up being excessively down on yourself when, in actual fact, an improvement from
100 to 86 in one year is to be applauded.

You must also make your goals specific. It is not enough to arrive on the 1st tee and hope
to 'hit a few more fairways', or 'hole a few more putts' than you did the last time you played.
If you missed a lot of fairways last time out and felt that was what influenced your score the
most, try to hit four or maybe five more fairways this time. This is not only more specific it is

realistic too. Improving from two fairways to 12 in one round, for example, is probably asking too much of yourself. Specifying your goals focuses the mind on the job in hand. Vague goals confuse the brain and lead to indecision.

VISUALIZE THE SHOT THEN ENGAGE AUTOPILOT

Eating, driving, tying your shoelaces. These are all activities you perform successfully without thinking about how you do them. In the car, for instance, you don't consciously think 'right foot down' if you want to increase your speed. And you certainly don't give any consideration to your technique when chewing or swallowing. Because you have carried out these actions thousands of times the movements come naturally.

What happens is your sub-conscious mind takes over and allows you to carry out the necessary functions to complete the task. In effect your body is on autopilot. And if you have played any amount of golf you will have discovered that you play your best when you have engaged autopilot and stopped thinking consciously about your swing. You will find if you hit your ball into a lake or forest off the tee, and then reload with a provisional ball, you will probably smack that one down the middle of the fairway. It happens almost without exception. But why? Because your mind has been cleared of all the 'how to's.' A problem occurs with the first swing because your head is full of technical clutter. You are

Visualize what you are trying to do, then just let it happen.

consciously thinking about how to swing the golf club. Your rhythm is inevitably affected and you fail to deliver a square clubface to the ball, hence the wayward shot. When you set up to the provisional, however, all you are concerned with is where you want the ball to go, not how to get it there. Suddenly your rhythm returns and you sweep through the ball which sails off into the distance.

Before going into autopilot mode, however, it is crucial you pre-program into your sub-conscious the shot you will be attempting to play. You do this by visualizing in your mind's eye everything you want to happen. As you stand behind the ball at the start of your pre-shot routine picture yourself making a smooth, balanced swing and the ball starting off on the exact trajectory and line you want it to start on. Continue the sequence to the point where the ball lands on the exact spot you want it to as you swing into a balanced follow through position. Run the sequence a few times in your imagination before walking up alongside your ball. Then just let it happen.

You rely on your sub-conscious a million times a day in bed, in your car, at the dinner table or just walking down the street. It keeps you safe and allows you to function at or near your best. You should learn to rely on it on the golf course too.

POSITIVE INTERNAL DIALOGUE

How can anyone possibly hope to perform well at any discipline if they are constantly cursing their bad luck or lack of ability? Negative thoughts are seriously hazardous to your golf and you should do everything in your power to stop them from creeping into your head. Your inner voice, or internal dialogue, must be

'I will hit this close, I will hit this close...'

positive. You shouldn't berate yourself for hooking your ball into the rough but tell yourself how you are going to escape from it and wind up with a par or bogey, not a triple bogey or worse.

Also, speak highly of your game to others. The tendency with beginners, and indeed all club golfers, is to inform their playing partners just prior to setting off of how badly they have been playing recently. The thinking is that when their game goes off the rails – normally straight away – it is not unexpected, and no one will be disappointed. Of course, by speaking of your bad form you only serve to extend the period of failure. So if you're shooting some high numbers and someone on the 1st tee asks you how you are playing tell them you've actually been striking the ball really well and that today that good ball striking is going to be converted into a good score. It may not work every time but you'll do a lot better than the guy who says he's playing rubbish and no doubt will again.

This is a simple but important lesson so **THINK POSITIVE AND SPEAK POSITIVE.**

ONE SHOT AT A TIME
A dangerous trap that amateur golfers often fall head first into is thinking forward to a pivotal hole they know they will face later in the round or thinking back to a bad shot they've already played. Thinking ahead to a tough, feature hole, a par-3 surrounded by water for instance, will only make it tougher when you eventually arrive there. Thinking back to a bad shot you've already played will only put negative thoughts in your head and diminish your chances of making a decent swing. You need to stay in the present, thinking not of what has gone or what is to come but what you are doing **NOW**.

If you finish a hole with a six or seven strike it from your memory and concentrate immediately on the next hole. Imagine that hole is the 1st and that you were hitting the ball well when warming up before the round. Once you hit a shot or complete a hole forget it. Whether you start your round 3,3,3 or 7,7,7 those previous scores should be irrelevant. Hit one shot at a time and as soon as you see your ball land start to think about what you are going to do with your next shot.

Often you will find that as your game improves and your scores start coming down you will be tempted to start calculating well before you reach the 18th tee what you need to do in order to beat your best ever score. This is one of the worst mental mistakes you can make as you will shatter the concentration you built up earlier in the round and introduce a million ifs and buts into your head. That can really only lead to disaster.

REMEMBER
1) Set yourself realistic and specific goals.
2) Pick a target, visualize the shot you want to play then let your autopilot take over.
3) Think and speak positively.
4) Play one shot at a time.

RULES AND ETIQUETTE

GOLF IS A GAME GOVERNED by many rules and various principles of etiquette. Before you start playing the game seriously, and certainly before you enter your first competition, it is important you have a reasonable grasp of these regulations. Failure to abide by them could lead to penalties or disqualification. So it's in your best interests to know when you have made an infringement and how, in some cases, you can use these rules to your advantage.

RULES TO REMEMBER

The Rules of golf are copious and complex to say the least. Only a handful of people on the planet, namely those that work in the rules departments of the game's governing bodies, The Royal and Ancient Golf Club of St Andrews (R&A) and the United States Golf Association (USGA), could ever claim to know them all off by heart. And even some of those gentlemen would need prompting from time to time.

In the official R&A Rules book there are, at present, 34 Rules, concerning everything from parts of the course to items of equipment. However, they are broken down into all sorts of sub-sections, appendices, clauses, definitions and exceptions. The resulting mass of information is one that no club golfer could be expected to memorize. Therefore, in order to simplify the Rules, I have concentrated only on those which will affect you most often.

You should always carry a Rules book with you on the course and you should also explain any situation about which you are unsure to a member of the Rules Committee of your golf club **BEFORE** you sign and hand in your scorecard. If you hand in your scorecard and it is later discovered that you breached a Rule in the course of the round you will be disqualified. You will also be disqualified if you mistakenly sign for a score that is, in fact, lower than your actual score. If, however, you mistakenly sign for a score that is higher than the score you actually shot the higher score remains.

DID YOU KNOW?

The most famous example of a player signing for an incorrect scorecard occurred at the 1968 US Masters. The Argentine golfer Roberto de Vincenzo made a birdie three on the 17th hole in the final round but his playing partner Tommy Aaron marked down a four by mistake. De Vincenzo failed to notice the error and signed his scorecard thus signing for a score higher than the score he actually achieved. Tragically, he missed out on a play-off by one shot.

14 CLUBS

Fourteen is the maximum number of clubs you are permitted in your bag. If you start with fewer than 14 you can add any number of clubs so that the new total becomes 14. You may also replace any club that becomes damaged but only if it was damaged in the normal course of play. Snapping a putter over your knee or demolishing the head of your driver by smacking it against a fence does not constitute the normal course of play so you won't be permitted to replace it.

You may share your clubs with your partner when playing foreballs or foursomes and he with you, only if the total number of clubs you are both carrying is not higher than 14.

Be warned. There have been numerous incidents of professional golfers having been disqualified from important tournaments for carrying an extra club.

PENALTY

In strokeplay if the number of clubs in your bag exceeds 14 you are penalized two strokes for every hole you played after the breach occurred, with a maximum penalty of four shots.

In matchplay you lose each hole you play after the breach occurred, with a maximum penalty of two holes.

If you notice you have 15 clubs in your bag you must declare one unplayable immediately and not use it again after that. Use the club declared unplayable again during the round and you will be disqualified.

Right: Under the Rules you are only permitted 14 clubs in your bag.

TEEING GROUND

As you read in chapter 1, the teeing ground is the place from which each hole starts. You are permitted to play your ball off the ground, off a tee peg or off some sand or other substance used to raise it off the ground. As for where to tee your ball up (and you should tee the ball up on every hole to give yourself the best lie possible) you may do so only between the two markers and up to two club lengths behind them. You may stand outside of the resulting rectangle to play a ball from within it.

If your ball falls off the tee before you start your swing you are allowed to tee it up again without penalty.

PENALTY

Playing your ball from outside the permitted teeing area carries a two stroke penalty in strokeplay. After imposing the penalty you must play another ball from the correct place. In matchplay, however, your opponent may insist that you play another shot from the right place without any further penalty to you.

You cannot tee up in front of the markers or more than two club lengths behind them.

PROVISIONAL BALL

If you hit a wayward shot into a thick forest or deep rough the chances are it will be lost. In this situation, to save time going and looking for it, you should hit what is called a provisional ball from the same spot you played the initial shot. You must inform your playing partners that the ball you are about to play is a provisional and then play it before you go ahead to look for the first ball. You can continue to hit the provisional ball until you reach the point where you think the first ball is lost. If you hit the provisional after that point, i.e. from closer to the hole than where the original ball is likely to be, you deem the original ball lost and the provisional becomes the ball in play. When you reach the area where the first ball is lost you have five minutes to look for it. If you fail to find it in that time the provisional automatically becomes the ball in play. You should follow the same procedure if you believe your ball finishes Out of Bounds.

PENALTY

If you fail to inform your opponent of your intention to hit a provisional, you deem the original ball lost and the ball you hit becomes the ball in play. You still count the stroke for the lost ball.

PLAYING OUT OF A HAZARD

GENERAL RULE

Any bunker or water feature is classed as a hazard. In a hazard your club is not allowed to make contact with the sand or water (called grounding the club) prior to playing the shot. That means you have to hover the clubhead above the surface when you are addressing the ball.

PENALTY

Two shots in strokeplay, loss of hole in matchplay.

Right: Do not let the clubhead touch the sand or water when you address the ball.

WATER HAZARD

A water hazard is any sea, ocean, lake, pond, stream or ditch that is a constant feature of the course. It is defined by yellow stakes or a painted yellow line and any ground or water within that yellow boundary is deemed to be within the hazard. That means if your ball is over the line but not in the water and you choose to play it as it lies you are not allowed to ground your club. A water hazard need not necessarily have water in it.

If your ball finishes in a water hazard you basically have three options for your next move.

1) Play the ball as it lies in the hazard.
2) Play another ball from where you played your last shot.
3) Drop a ball behind the water hazard, keeping the point at which the ball last crossed the margin of the hazard directly between you and the hole. You can go back as far as you like on that line.

PENALTY

There is no penalty for taking option 1, however you must add one stroke to your score if you take options 2 or 3.

You can play it as it lies in a water hazard if you wish...but don't ground your club.

You may be better off replaying the original shot (left) or dropping the ball away from the hazard (above).

If you decide you can play the ball from within the hazard but you fail to get it out with your next shot you can choose from another three options. Either play it from where it comes to rest, or under a one stroke penalty choose option 3 above, or play a new ball from the position where you played the shot that went into the hazard originally.

LATERAL WATER HAZARD

A lateral water hazard is similar to a water hazard, the difference being it is situated in a position that would make dropping a ball behind it impractical. Lateral water hazards are defined by red stakes and usually run alongside a hole.

   If your ball lands in a lateral water hazard you have one additional possible course of action. You are allowed to drop a ball within two club lengths from the point where it last crossed the margin of the hazard or on a spot equidistant from the hole on the opposite side of the hazard. You must not drop the ball nearer the hole.

PENALTY

If you drop a ball out of the hazard you must add a stroke to your score.

In a lateral water hazard another option is to drop a ball within two club lengths of the point where it crossed the margin of the hazard.

IMMOVABLE OBSTRUCTION

An immovable obstruction is basically any fixed object on the course, such as a greenkeeper's hut, halfway house or rain shelter. If your stance or the intended area of your swing is interfered with by an immovable obstruction you have to find the nearest point of the course where the obstruction no longer affects your stance or swing (the nearest point of relief). You should then drop a ball within one club length of that spot making sure the ball lands no nearer the hole. If you are in a bunker you must drop the ball within the bunker.

PENALTY

There is no penalty for dropping away from an immovable obstruction.

If there is reasonable evidence to suggest your ball is lost within an immovable obstruction you can substitute another ball and drop it within one club length from the point at which it entered the obstruction, again making sure it doesn't land nearer the hole. There is no penalty.

You can drop away without penalty from this situation.

MOVABLE OBSTRUCTION

If you watch golf on television you often see golf balls come to rest on spectator's belongings or their litter. These objects, along with items such as bunker rakes and discarded scorecards are seen as movable obstructions. If your ball lies close to such an object you are allowed to remove the obstruction. If however, in moving the obstruction, your ball moves you are allowed to replace it without penalty, provided the movement of the ball was caused unintentionally by the removal of the obstruction.

PENALTY

If you move the ball in any way other than by removing the obstruction you will be penalized one stroke.

You can move the rake. If the ball moves replace it in its original position.

LOOSE IMPEDIMENT

Any naturally occurring object such as a stone, leaf, twig, animal dropping, insect, worm, or worm cast is regarded as a loose impediment, as long as the object is not fixed or growing, is not solidly embedded and does not stick to the ball. Sand and loose soil are regarded as loose impediments but only on the green.

You are allowed to remove any loose impediment from the area around your ball.

PENALTY

If your ball moves while you are removing an impediment that lies within one club length of your ball you must add a stroke to your score. You must then replace it. If you move your ball, or marker, while removing a loose impediment on the green, however, there is no penalty.

When removing a loose impediment take care not to move the ball.

UNPLAYABLE BALL

Whenever your ball is lodged in a place such as the trunk of a tree or in waist-high rough, you really should think twice before trying to hit it. You are perfectly entitled to hit it, of course, but you are more than likely to break your club and probably your hands and wrists too. Your wisest move is to declare the ball unplayable, which you can do at any place on the course except when your ball is in a water hazard. If you do decide your ball is unplayable you can:

1) Go back to where you played your last shot and add one stroke to your score. (If that

shot was played from the tee you can tee your ball up anywhere within the teeing ground, if it was 'through the green' [the term given to all areas of the course between 'the tee' and 'the green'] you have to drop it, and if it was on the green you have to place your ball).

2) Drop your ball within two club lengths of the spot where the ball lies but not nearer the hole, or

3) Drop your ball as far back as you like from the point where the ball lies, keeping that point directly between you and the hole.

If your ball is unplayable in a bunker — it might be lodged in the grass rivet face for instance — you must drop your ball in the bunker if you choose to follow the second or third of the above options.

PENALTY

If you breach this rule in any way you will be penalized two shots in strokeplay and you will lose the hole if you're playing matchplay.

Play it if you like but you are probably better off replaying from the original spot or dropping clear.

HITTING YOURSELF, PARTNER OR OPPONENT WITH YOUR BALL

Rule 19, which deals with the accidental deflecting or stopping of a ball by outside agencies (referees, markers, spectators), yourself and your opponent, is one of the more complex in the Rule book.

Basically, if your ball hits an outside agency, while in motion, the Rules clearly state this is a rub of the green and there is no penalty. The ball should then be played from where it lies.

If it deflects off yourself, your partner or any part of your equipment (or either of your caddies should you have them) you incur a penalty of two shots in strokeplay or loss of hole in matchplay. Again, play the ball from where it finishes. If you hit your opponent or his equipment (or his caddie if he has one) on the other hand there is no penalty. You can then either play the ball as it lies or, before another shot is played by either player, cancel that stroke and play another from the spot where you last played.

Oops. If the person in red is your opponent there is no penalty and you can either continue, or play it again. If he's your partner or caddie it's a two stroke penalty.

MARKING AND CLEANING YOUR BALL

You are allowed to mark, lift and clean your ball any time you are on the green. Lifting and cleaning on the fairway is also permissible during periods when Winter Rules are in place. Winter Rules allow you to mark the position of your ball on the fairway, pick it up, clean it and replace it within six inches of where it was originally but not nearer the hole. You may also mark and lift your ball anywhere on the course in order to identify it, determine if it is unfit for use or if it is interfering with, or assisting, play.

To mark your ball, place your ball marker or coin as closely behind it as possible without it moving. Then replace it on the exact spot from which you lifted it. If your ball marker is on the line of your opponent's putt he may ask you to move it. To do this mark off one putterhead's

Mark the position of your ball with a ball marker or coin. You may then clean it.

length from your marker in the direction of a tree or other fixed landmark off the green. Then replace your marker at the toe end of the putterhead. Remember to replace your marker in its proper position when it's your turn to putt.

PENALTY

If you lift and clean your ball when not permitted to do so you incur a penalty of one stroke.

REPAIRING PITCH MARKS AND SPIKE MARKS

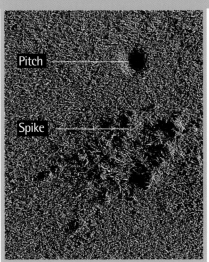

Pitch

Spike

You are allowed to repair any pitch mark (an indentation on the surface caused by the impact of a ball) even if your ball is not actually on the green. You are not allowed to repair any other kind of damage to the green prior to hitting your putt, however. Damage caused by spikes must, therefore, remain untouched.

PENALTY

If you repair any damage on the green made by anything other than the impact of a ball you suffer a two stroke penalty in strokeplay and you automatically lose the hole in matchplay.

CASUAL WATER

After a heavy downpour your ball may come to rest in an area where the rain water has not permeated the surface. This is called casual water and is not to be regarded as a water hazard. You can play the ball as it lies if you want but the wiser move would be to determine the nearest spot to your ball which is unaffected by the water and not nearer the hole. You can then lift, clean and drop it within one club length of that spot.

If the casual water lies on the green and affects the line of your putt you can replace your ball in the nearest point of relief from the water and not nearer the hole. There is no penalty for dropping or replacing your ball in this situation.

Note that dew and frost are not deemed casual water but snow is. Also, you are allowed to take relief if the ball is on dry land but your stance is affected by the condition.

Find the nearest point of relief from casual water and drop within one club length of that, not nearer the hole.

PENALTY

Any breach of this Rule (Rule 25) will lead to a two stroke penalty in strokeplay and the loss of the hole in matchplay.

NB In an attempt to make these Rules sound less complex than they do in the official Rule book, which is produced by the Royal and Ancient Golf Club, I have paraphrased them. Sometimes that can lead to important points being lost in the translation. Therefore, please be sure to consult with an official R&A Rule book or your club's Rules Committee if you are in any doubt at all over the correct procedure in a certain situation.

ETIQUETTE

One of the reasons golf is so special, and there are many, is because its enthusiasts abide by a code of conduct that engenders a unique sense of fair play. In no other sport will you find amateurs and top professionals sticking to the Rules or calling penalties on themselves - penalties which could ultimately cost them important titles – in the way golfers do. But it's not just this respect for the Rules that sets golf and golfers apart from other sportsmen. The laws of etiquette, which basically deal with how a golfer should behave towards his opponent, and also how he can help maintain the course in the best condition possible, are an integral part of the game. Golf etiquette is global and not just a bunch of archaic and irrelevant laws a group of aristocratic Scots created in the middle of the 18th century to keep golf a game for the privileged minority.

As with every other aspect of the game, the more you play the more you will learn. However, it is imperative you have a good grounding in the laws of etiquette before you play golf for the first time and make a habit of applying them as soon as possible.

CARE OF THE COURSE

REPLACE DIVOTS

It is extremely annoying to hit a lifetime's best drive down the middle of the fairway only to find your ball in a divot. To prevent those following you from having to play out of your divots and to help the grass take root again, you must replace them immediately. Retrieve as much of the grass taken as possible and stamp it down into the hole that has been created.

REPAIR PITCH MARKS

When your ball lands on the green it will probably make an indentation on the surface. This indentation is called a pitch mark and otherwise excellent greens can be ruined by pitch marks that go unrepaired. Make it a habit every time you walk on to a green of repairing your own pitch mark and one other. That way you will be doing your bit to keep the greens looking great and putting smoothly.

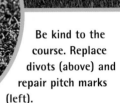

Be kind to the course. Replace divots (above) and repair pitch marks (left).

Also, to fully ensure you leave the green looking as good as it did when you walked on to it, take care when removing the flag and placing it on the ground and don't lean too heavily on your putter.

RAKE BUNKERS

Hitting a lousy shot into a sand trap and discovering your ball in a large footprint left by a player in the group ahead is rubbing salt into the wound. It makes your shot infinitely more difficult than it already is, a penalty which could have been so easily avoided. Every time, and I mean every time, you play out of a bunker use the rake — there should be one nearby — to smooth over your footprints. It should only take a minute to do properly. Leave the bunker how you would like to find it.

It doesn't hurt, doesn't cost anything and takes less than a minute – so do it!

PRACTICE SWINGS

When executing an actual stroke, especially with a short iron, it is sometimes inevitable that you will take a divot. That's perfectly acceptable, of course. However, it is extremely bad etiquette to damage the course unnecessarily by removing large divots when making practice swings, especially on teeing grounds. If a couple of practice swings are part of your pre-shot routine go to the side of the tee and do them there. You thus eliminate the risk of damaging the turf excessively.

ALSO:

1) Don't drop your bag on a green or teeing ground. Place it to the side.

2) Obey any signs that give instructions on where you can and can't pull your trolley or drive your buggy.

3) Many golf clubs put boxes of earth and grass seed next to the teeing grounds of short holes. If there is such a box on the hole you are playing help the greenkeeper out by filling your divot with some of the mixture provided.

Help keep the teeing ground looking good by making practice swings to the side of it.

COURTESY ON THE COURSE

If you walk briskly you will have longer to play your next shot. Never hold up players behind you.

BE QUIET

This is perhaps the most obvious law of etiquette. It is simply common courtesy to allow your opponent/partner to play his shot in silence. Making any sort of noise while he is in the process of playing the stroke and you are likely to disturb his concentration. Don't stand too close to him when he is playing and don't stand directly behind him either.

PACE OF PLAY

Nothing spoils a round of golf like having to wait on every shot for the group ahead to clear the fairway or green. If you lose a hole on the match ahead (a gap of one hole opens up between you and them) you must allow the group following you to play through.

Always play without delay. Here are some simple hints to ensure you don't hold up play:

1) Don't mark your scorecard on the green of the hole you've just completed. Leave the green immediately after holing out and do it on the next tee while those you are playing with hit their tee shots (the person who had the lowest score on the previous hole has 'the honour' on the next tee and plays first).

2) Walk briskly between shots. You will then have all the time in the world (well within reason) to decide on a club, what shot you want to play and then play it.

3) If you have to search for a ball that is lost do not wait the five minutes in which you are allowed to look for it to pass before calling through the group behind. Call them through as soon as it becomes apparent it will take some time to find it.

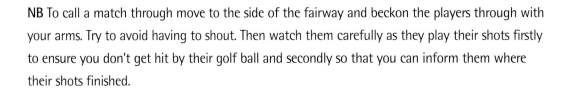

4) You should always wait for the group ahead to get out of range before you hit your shot but don't wait until they are 350 yards away if the furthest you've ever hit a golf ball is 200 yards.

5) Put your bag on the side of the green that is closest to the next tee (right). Don't just drop it at the front of the green. This will allow the group behind to play their shots without having to wait for you to collect your bag.

Remember, it's not enough just to stay ahead of the group behind. You should try to keep up with the group in front.

NB To call a match through move to the side of the fairway and beckon the players through with your arms. Try to avoid having to shout. Then watch them carefully as they play their shots firstly to ensure you don't get hit by their golf ball and secondly so that you can inform them where their shots finished.

RYDER CUP CONFLICT

A well documented breach of etiquette by professional golfers occurred at the 1999 Ryder Cup played at Brookline, Massachusetts, USA. Late on Sunday afternoon with the outcome of the match still firmly in the balance, Justin Leonard, representing the USA, and Jose Maria Olazabal, representing Europe, came to the 17th hole all square. Leonard found the green in regulation (two shots) but left himself a treacherous 50 foot putt. Olazabal was slightly closer in two. The green was ringed by a huge gallery which included most of the players and their wives. If Leonard could somehow hole his putt and Olazabal miss his it would mean Leonard could not lose his match and the USA would win the cup back from Europe, which had won the biennial contest in 1995 and 1997. The tension was considerable but Leonard broke it when he rolled his

putt in to the obvious delight of the partisan galleries. Not to put too fine a point on it, all hell broke loose. The American players and their wives invaded the green, some walking all over the line of Olazabal's putt. Given the competitive nature of the Ryder Cup, this uninhibited display of emotion was perfectly understandable, but, considering Olazabal still had a putt to keep the match alive, also deeply regrettable.

ON THE GREEN

Four pointers for good etiquette on the greens:

1) Never stand directly behind your opponent or the hole when he is putting.

2) Be very careful not to walk on the line of your opponent's putt as you will spike up the grass between his ball and the hole if you do.

3) Do not cast your shadow over your opponent's line, his ball as he is addressing it, or the hole.

4) Offer to attend the flag when your partner/opponent is putting.

CONCLUSION

Perhaps it's not that difficult after all, this golf lark. Don't let anyone tell you otherwise and don't, whatever you do, get bogged down in searching for perfection. Golf has existed for several hundred years and no one has found it yet. So what makes you think you can?

Always remember you will play your best golf when you aren't really thinking about how to swing the club. That's in the future though. First you have to do a little conscious work on your fundamentals. If you get them right, do your fair share of practice and then let your friendly autopilot, who resides somewhere deep inside your sub-conscious, take over, you WILL play good golf sooner or later.

Good luck and **HAVE FUN!**

ACKNOWLEDGEMENTS

The pictures for this book were shot at Tat Beach Golf Club and Nobilis Golf Club in Antalya, Turkey. Many thanks to Alternative Travel (London) for arranging the photo shoot and sincere thanks also to Ayhan Karaagaÿ (Tat Beach) and John Nolan (Nobilis) for their help in seeing that all ran smoothly.

The suppliers of the equipment were;
Taylor Made: Clubs
Dunlop: Balls
Izzo: Bag
Ashworth: Clothes
Stylo: Shoes

PICTURE CREDITS

All photographs courtesy of Bob Atkins unless otherwise stated.
Allsport: 14 (bottom), 25 (bottom), 55 (bottom),
67, 72, 87, 96 (top), 142 (bottom)